THE CHICKASAW BAYOU CAMPAIGN

by

GRAY M. GILDNER, MAJ, USA

U.S. Army Command and General Staff College

Fort Leavenworth, Kansas

1991

Table of Contents

The opinions and conclusions expressed herein are those of the student author and do not necessarily represent the views of the U.S. Army Command and General Staff College or any other governmental agency.

INTRODUCTION

By December 1862, Union efforts to defeat the Confederacy had met with limited success and many, many failures. In the Eastern Theater of Operations the Union Army of the Potomac had been repeatedly defeated but, even when successful, its various commanding generals did not have the ability or strength of will to pursue the Army of Northern Virginia to a conclusive victory. In the Western Theater Union fortunes were radically different. Union forces were led by the best officers to emerge in the war. Union offensive campaigns had sent the Confederate western armies reeling to the south and the only substantial obstacle to Union control on the Mississippi River lay in the seizure of Vicksburg.

The Chickasaw Bayou Campaign from December 1862 to January 1863 was the first major effort by Union forces to seize the city of Vicksburg. The campaign initiated by Major General Ulysses S. Grant sent an amphibious force under Major General William T. Sherman from Memphis, Tennessee, down the Mississippi River, while the remainder of Grant's forces pinned the Confederate army under Lieutenant General John C. Pemberton in north central Mississippi. The complete failure of the campaign and the magnitude of the subsequent Union triumphs have so overshadowed the event that military and Civil War historians have taken little notice of it and have exerted little effort to conduct a detailed campaign analysis. Nevertheless, the clearly defined strategic, operational, tactical, and joint characteristics of the campaign mark it as an excellent source for military study.

At the strategic level the military and political activities surrounding the campaign were significant features in both the Union and Confederacy. The campaigns to control the Mississippi River were the most strategically important in the Western Theater during the Civil War. Some of the most influential military and political leaders of the war were involved in the planning and coordination of both the Union and Confederate operations. For example, the Union campaigns were the direct result of President Abraham Lincoln's preeminence in the development of national military strategy. The execution of his strategic designs was left to Secretary of War Edwin M. Stanton and, eventually, General-In-Chief Henry W. Halleck, both of whose influences would be seen in the Chickasaw Bayou Campaign. The Confederate strategic planning and execution offer similarities. President Jefferson C. Davis formulated and closely controlled the Confederate national military strategy. The problems of implementation of his strategy through several Secretaries of War and generals in

2

the field are exemplified in this campaign.

Intertwined with the strategic and operational elements of this campaign are the exceptional influences of personalities and politics. The operational planning of the Union was an outstanding example of perceived and real interference by civilian authority in military matters. While Grant fought the battles in the Mississippi valley with the object of controlling the river, President Lincoln and Secretary Stanton were supporting their own autonomous effort to seize Vicksburg by an amphibious assault. This effort, to be lead by a former politician, Major General John A. McClernand, makes the analysis of this campaign particularily peculiar and therefore interesting.

The operation was very sophisticated, even by later standards. Immense Union forces operated in a massive theater of war hampered by primitive communications, primitive roads, and trackless wilderness. Union forces conducted complicated joint naval and army operations on a scale never previously seen or contemplated. The campaign exemplifies many of the problems of command common to both the Union and Confederacy at that stage of the war.

The campaign culminated with the seemingly futile battle at Chickasaw Bayou where Union forces attempted repeatedly to dislodge entrenched Confederate defenders in frontal assaults. The conduct of the battle led to charges for decades after the war. Led by Union General George W. Morgan and Confederate General Stephen D. Lee, postwar literature was highly critical of Sherman, Grant, and other Union battle leaders.

No single event can be identified which in particular resulted in the outcome at Chickasaw Bayou. A cursory study of the campaign can identify a number of obvious events at the strategic, operational, and tactical level of the campaign which contributed to the defeat of the Union operation. The determination of the decisive factors at each of those levels requires substantial analysis. The lessons that can be derived from the determination of these factors are the essence of the study of military operations.

At the strategic level the campaign was affected by the Union inability to establish a unified commander for the departments in the Mississippi River region of the Western Theater. This lack of a unified commander for all operations on the Mississippi River was a constant thorn in Grant's side. Far more destructive was the havoc created by the assignment of McClernand by Lincoln to a seperate command in Grant's own department. This assignment, without question, prematurely energized Grant's ill fated Chickasaw Bayou campaign. The Confederate command structure in the months prior to

Chickasaw Bayou was in a shambles, the leadership materially contributing to the sad outcome of the Confederate defensive campaigns. In the weeks prior to the Chickasaw Bayou campaign the whole Confederate command structure was reorganized. The effect of this shake up was instrumental in the successful defense.

The most conspicuous factors leading to the outcome at Chickasaw Bayou are at the operational level. Two Confederate cavalry raids destroyed Grant's railroad line of communications and stopped Grant's overland manuevers. Grant, unable to conceive that he could campaign without strong lines of communications, stopped dead in his tracks, failing completely to support Sherman. Without any Union action in central Mississippi Pemberton skillfully maneuvered scarce reserves to defeat Sherman at Chickasaw Bayou. Additionally, Pemberton's defensive preparations were simplified by the failure of the Union commanders to deceive the enemy. Although the marshalling of the huge river force could not be shielded from enemy spies, concealing the exact timing and location of the attack was well within their capablities. Confederate commanders at Vicksburg had been lulled into a sense of security due to the routine sorties of river boats and gunboats over a period of months. The tremendous increase in the activity of the gunboats in the days prior to the landing at

Chickasaw Bayou served only to pinpoint the exact location of the assault.

As a result of the disasters to Grant's forces in central Mississippi, and the total lack of surprise created by the naval operations, Sherman's battle at Chickasaw Bayou appeared unwinnable from the moment he landed. This is not the case. With all the factors benefiting the Confederate ability to react to the Union operation, Pemberton still lacked any forces of consequence at the Bayou when Sherman landed. What forces were available frantically fortified and positioned themselves to stall Sherman while he cautiously inched forward. Sherman, with forces that could have overwhelmed the initial Confederate defenders disposed against him, made no major attack against the Confederates until four days after landing. On the other hand, the Confederate sense of purpose in reinforcing the Bayou area shattered Sherman's final chances.

In the final analysis the ultimate failure of the Chickasaw Bayou campaign may be attributed to the actions of Major General U.S. Grant and Lieutenant General John C. Pemberton. Grant failed completely to support the amphibious wing under Sherman. Regardless of the raids to his rear, he had an obligation to pin Pemberton's army in central Mississippi. Without this support Sherman lost the key to the operation. Pemberton, although criticized for his failure in later campaigns, can be credited with the decisive Confederate counterstrokes. Pemberton devised, coordinated, and unleashed the dual cavalry raids into Grant's rear. It was Pemberton who reorganized the defenses in north central Mississippi and in Vicksburg and organized the decisive reinforcement at Chickasaw Bayou.

CHAPTER ONE - STRATEGIC SETTING

Ordered that the 22d day of February 1862, be the day
for a general movement of the Land and Naval forces
of the United States against the insurgent forces.
Abraham Lincoln, 27 Jan 1862[1]

UNION WAR STRATEGY

President Lincoln's ultimate objective in the Civil War
was the restoration of the Union. The Union strategic plans
required seizure of significant portions of the Confederacy
literally to exhaust them into submission. This plan, therefore,
required Union forces to take the offensive. The strategy
embarked on by President Lincoln in 1861 focused Union
efforts in the Eastern and Western theaters of war. Enclosed
within these theaters of war were three major axes of attack
into the Confederacy.[2] The Western Theater encompassed the
Mississippi River axis and the axis of advance to break the
Allegheny barrier. The Eastern Theater of war enclosed the
drive to seize Richmond.

The Union attacks to seize control of the Mississippi
River developed into two theaters of operation with Union
forces attacking north and south along the river axis. The
southern Mississippi River theater of operations began with the
seizure of New Orleans on 1 May 1862 and ended with the
capture of Fort Hudson on 9 July 1863. Operations in the

northern Mississippi River theater of operations began with the battle of Mill Spring, Kentucky, in January 1862 and Ft. Henry, Tennessee, and Ft. Donelson, Tennessee, in February 1862. It culminated with the seizure of Vicksburg on 4 July 1863.[3]

The were three purposes for the offensive in the Mississippi valley. The primary purpose was to reestablish Union navigation on the river, and open the markets of the Union western states to the eastern United States and Europe.[4] The closure of the Mississippi River was a significant economic burden to the western states and added to the challenges of maintaining support for the war.[5]

The second element of the strategy was to prevent the Trans-Mississippi region of the Confederacy from supporting the eastern Confederacy. This region was a tremendous source of foodstuffs, and offered an excellent means of communications through Mexico to Europe.[6] Finally, by splitting the Confederacy along the Mississippi River, the Union could concentrate forces on the strongest section and defeat it. The isolated Trans-Mississippi region of the Confederacy would fall as a result of the destruction of the eastern Confederacy.[7]

The second major Union offensive axis in the Western Theater was the advance from Kentucky through middle and east Tennessee designed to break the Allegheny barrier at

Chattanooga, Tennessee. Actions within this theater of operations were designed to penetrate the Confederate heartland in order to allow Union forces to flank Confederate eastern forces.[8]

The third Union offensive axis was the advance from Washington, D.C., along the eastern coast with the object of seizing Richmond. This theater would be the focus of Union resources and attention until well into the war. Similarly, the South concentrated its efforts in the east due to the dominant position of Virginia and Richmond in the minds of southerners.[9]

In conjunction with the enormous ground offensives, the U.S. Navy would conduct blockades, capture ports, and conduct expeditions along the coast. The intent was to draw off Confederate forces and assets, and isolate the South from international markets.[10]

CONFEDERATE WAR STRATEGY

Confederate strategic plans were never as clearly defined as the Union's. This was largely the result of the personality of President Jefferson Davis and the unique aspects of the Confederacy. Davis understood the Union objective of restoring the Union through the strategy of exhaustion. As a result, he sought to conduct a strategic defense to wear down the Union will to conduct the war, to prevent loss of Confederate territory, and to allow time for foreign recognition and intervention.[11]

Most influential Confederate leaders agreed to the strategic defense. They clearly understood that the loss of territory would contribute to the loss of important resources as well as prestige in the eyes of foreign powers. Furthermore, they understood that the Union could not be overwhelmed, but would have to be bloodied to the point of losing the will to continue. The actual operational methods for the conduct of the strategic defense caused the greatest tensions and problems between the generals in the field and Davis.

The nature of the Confederacy forced Davis into an inflexible doctrine of defending every threatened point. Every Union foray onto Confederate soil brought pleas for assistance from Confederate governors. The link between the Confederate government in Richmond and the highly individualistic Confederate states was never firm and necessitated a policy of territorial defense.[12] The outcome of this defense was a weakening of every army in the field as units were frittered away in the defense of strategically unimportant regions. The necessity to guard everything lead the Confederacy to lose the initiative by having no definitive plans. When asked what Davis's strategic plans were for the crisis, Secretary of War

James A. Seddon replied that he did not have one and never had any.[13] Davis reacted to crises as they arose.

The opposing school of thought among the Confederate leadership called for the concentration of Confederate forces on a national level to counter the major Union offensives driving southward. The solution which resulted from this debate was the recognition of the importance of all territory, with some concentration of forces on the theater level. The concentration of forces, however, was normally associated with specific reactions to Union offensives and not on any long term or planned basis.[14]

THE WESTERN THEATER

In the planning and conduct of offensive operations in the Western Theater, Union commanders were compelled by the physical characteristics of the region to consider factors completely unimportant in any other theater of operations. The lines of operations of Union armies depended on the availablity of rivers, railroads, and railheads. Campaigns focused on control of these critical networks with the enemy army often of secondary importance. Control of these limited assets destroyed the enemy army's ability to sustain itself in the vast region.

Rivers were major factors in Civil War operations. In the Eastern Theater, rivers flowed east to west, thus becoming significant obstacles to Union offensives into the south. In the Western Theater, the key rivers ran north to south. This characteristic provided significant advantages to the Union and resulted in immense naval operations to take advantage of the water systems. Union military forces in every western campaign were inextricably linked to the river currently being used to drive southward. The operational significance of the rivers can be seen in the naming of the Union armies of the Civil War. Whereas the Army of the Potomac stagnated for years in seesaw battles along that river, western armies moved progressively forward often requiring combination into new formations. These new formations became associated by name to the established river lines of communications.

Unlike the Eastern Theater where railroads and road networks abounded, the Western Theater was still a wilderness in the early 1860's. Railroad systems were scarce and supported by very few railheads. Roads of the type found in the east were virtually nonexistent. Campaigns in the west focused on the all important and terribly limited railroad lines to augment operations on the rivers. If a railroad line could not be controlled, the offensive operations ceased. The tyranny of the rail lines was evident on 15 November 1862 when General Grant at LaGrange, Tennessee, arranged to meet General Sherman based in Memphis. Although only fifty miles separated them, the linking Memphis-Charleston Railroad was out of commission, and no adequate roads existed. Grant had to travel to Columbus, Kentucky, via the Tennessee and Ohio Railroad while Sherman took a boat up the Mississippi River in order to conduct their planning meeting, a diversion of several hundred miles.[15]

CAMPAIGNING IN THE WEST

Confederate defensive preparations in the Western Theater were solidified in September 1861 with the appointment of General Albert S. Johnston to command Department Number Two. This department was the principal western department and included Tennessee, Arkansas, Kentucky, Missouri, Kansas, and the western part of Mississippi. The main supporting department was Department Number One, oriented on the defense of New Orleans and commanded by Major General Mansfield Lovell. Additionally, Major General Braxton Bragg commanded a district encompassing Pensacola, Florida, and Mobile, Alabama. General A.S. Johnston organized his army into three wings to defend along the frontier and a separate, smaller force under Major General Earl Van Dorn in Arkansas. The left wing of Johnston's army was commanded by Major General Leonidas Polk, the right wing under Johnston himself, and the extreme right wing under Brigadier General Felix K. Zollicoffer.[16]

In November 1861 Union western forces were organized into the Army of the Mississippi under Major General Henry Halleck and the Army of the Ohio under Major General Don Carlos Buell. Buell initiated offensive operations with a victory over Zollicoffer's forces at Mill Spring, Kentucky, on 19 January 1862. Spurred into action by Buell's offensive, Halleck ordered Grant to seize Ft. Henry on the Tennessee River. With the assistance of gunboats, Grant seized the abandoned Ft. Henry and followed the Confederates to Ft. Donelson on the Cumberland River. Grant captured the fort with over 12,000 prisoners and thereby gained control of the Tennessee and Cumberland Rivers.[17]

The two Union offensives ruptured the Confederate center and threatened to turn the extreme right flank. Johnston was forced to evacuate western and central Tennessee, abandoning Nashville to Buell's advancing army. Johnston lead his force southeast through Tennessee and west through Alabama to Corinth, Mississippi, finally arriving on 22 March 1862. At Corinth he linked up with reinforcements rushed from Virginia under the command of General Pierre G.T. Beauregard.

The collapse of the Confederate center forced Polk on the left wing to retreat from Columbus, Kentucky, closely followed by an autonomous Union army under Major General John Pope. By the end of March, Pope's army was facing Island Number 10 on the Mississippi River just to the north of Memphis. Grant's and Buell's forces, under the overall command of Halleck since 11 March, were continuing to advance slowly southward.[18]

The Confederacy was in a desperate situation. Union advances to Corinth threatened the most strategically important town west of Chattanooga. Corinth was the rail head of the two critical railroads, the north-south Mobile and Ohio Railroad, and the east-west Memphis and Charleston Railroad. The Memphis and Charleston Railroad was the only east to west lateral north of Vicksburg for the Confederacy. The Confederate Secretary of War Leroy P. Walker described it as "the vertebrae of the Confederacy."[19] Johnston marshalled every Confederate force available at Corinth and brought Van Dorn's Arkansas force across the Mississippi River. Similarly, Halleck concentrated his forces near Pittsburg Landing in Tennessee for a drive toward Corinth. Before Buell's slow moving army arrived, Johnston surprised Grant's army at Shiloh on 6 April. In the ensuing battle, Johnston was killed and his deputy, General Beauregard, retreated after a bloody repulse. The Union "victory" lead to Halleck's assumption of active field command and the temporary ouster of Grant from command.[20]

Halleck began a deliberate and exceedingly slow advance against the retreating Confederates. By 30 May, Beauregard had retreated out of Corinth and moved his army back to Tupelo, Mississippi. In May a naval expedition under Rear Admiral David G. Farragut defeated Major General Lovell and seized New Orleans. By June, the Confederacy had lost Island Number 10, Ft Pillow, and Memphis to General Pope.[21] The two axes on the Mississippi had formed.

At the height of success in the west, the Union offensive stopped dead in its tracks. Halleck dispersed his command from Corinth. Pope was called east to command the Army of the Potomac and his western army was reallocated. Buell's Army of the Ohio slowly moved east towards Chattanooga, repairing the Memphis-Charleston Railroad enroute. Sherman later wrote in his memoirs: "Had he (Halleck) held his force as a unit, he could have gone to Mobile, or Vicksburg or anywhere in that region, which would by one move have solved the whole Mississippi problem."[22] Through June and July, Halleck's army remained dispersed along the Memphis-Charleston line between Memphis and Chattanooga. Confederate forces, in terrible disarray, reconstituted and prepared to fight another day.

While Halleck languished in Corinth, the naval and

army forces in New Orleans did not rest. Farragut quickly organized an expedition of nine ocean going war vessels, seventeen mortar boats, and troop transports to assault Vicksburg. Major General Benjamin F. Butler, commander of Army forces in New Orleans, did not support adequately the project, providing only 3,000 soldiers. The fleet arrived at Vicksburg on 18 May 1862 and demanded the city's surrender. The Confederates declined and Farragut began a softening bombardment lasting through June. On 28 June, Farragut's fleet ran the batteries north to link up with the Mississippi gunboat fleet from Cairo, Illinois, under Rear Admiral Charles H. Davis. It was clear to Farragut that he could not take Vicksburg alone.[23] On 23 June Secretary of War Stanton requested Halleck to try to support the naval expedition with his own forces.[24] Halleck replied that he had no force available but would "give the matter very full attention as circumstances will permit."[25] By 14 July, pressure on the Secretary of War by Secretary of the Navy Gideon Welles required Stanton again to seek Halleck's assistance.[26] Halleck again stated he could not provide any ground forces for Vicksburg.[27]

On 15 July, the Confederate gunboat <u>Arkansas</u> steamed out of the Yazoo River fighting its way through to Vicksburg. That night Farragut, frustrated at his inability to seize Vicksburg or even destroy a lone rebel raider, gave up his effort and returned to New Orleans. Farragut's expedition proved the futility of seizing Vicksburg with anything other than massive superiority on land and on the river. By failing to support the effort against Vicksburg, Halleck lost the last real chance to seize Vicksburg easily.

The expedition did have a useful consequence; it highlighted the abilities of Commander David D. Porter, a naval officer to be instrumental in Union naval operations for the remainder of the war. Commander Porter had conceived the plan to move up the Mississippi from New Orleans, had won Lincoln's approval to attempt it, and had commanded the mortar boats in the attack. The experience would be invaluable in his later river operations.

During the relative lull in campaigning in June and July 1862, both Union and Confederate forces conducted major reorganizations. Union forces began a period of confusing reorganization which would not be fixed for the remainder of the year. On 11 July 1862, Halleck was called to Washington to assume responsibilities as Union General-in-Chief. Calling the recently resurrected Grant to his headquarters, Halleck passed to him responsibility for the Army of the Mississippi. Although the two men were together at Corinth for two days, Halleck gave him no guidance as to the employment of the forces. Furthermore, Grant was given responsibility for the Army of the Mississippi and the Army of the Tennessee without the command of the Department of the Mississippi. This was a symptom of a typical lack of organizational ability on Halleck's part and was not corrected until Grant was assigned to command the newly created Department of Tennessee on 16 October 1862. Until then, Grant controlled only those forces in west Tennessee and Kentucky west of the Cumberland River.[28] Operating to Grant's west was the Army of the Missouri under Major General Samuel R. Curtis. To his east, also not under Grant's control, was the Army of the Ohio under General Buell. Halleck had created a gap in the command structure and damaged the unity of effort previously established in the west.

With the force at hand Grant defended for the remainder of the summer awaiting promised reinforcements. Grant held two divisions, the left wing of the Army of the Mississippi at Corinth, Rienzi, Jacinto, and Danville under the command of Brigadier General William S. Rosecrans. The center was commanded by Major General Edward O.C. Ord and extended from Bethel to Humboldt on the Mobile-Ohio Railroad and from Jackson to Bolivar. The right wing commanded by Major General Sherman was positioned in Memphis.[29]

As with Grant, Beauregard received no campaign guidance, complaining to the Confederate War Department that:

Since the battle of Shiloh, when I assumed command of the Western Department ... no instructions from the War Department relative to the policy of the government and the movements of the armies of the Confederacy have been received by me.[30]

On 20 June General Braxton Bragg replaced Beauregard as commander of Department Number 2 and assumed command of the combined Departments 1 and 2. At the beginning of July, Bragg reorganized his command into the Department of Mississippi under Major General Van Dorn and the Department of the Gulf under Brigadier General John H. Forney. The Army of the West was assigned to Major General Sterling Price and the Army of the Mississippi was placed under Major General William J. Hardee.[31] The Confederate forces west of the Mississippi were reorganized into the Department of the Trans-Mississippi under Lieutenant General Theophilus H. Holmes. Confederate forces to the east of Bragg in Major General E. Kirby Smith's Department of East Tennessee, though technically separate, were subordinated to Bragg for operations. Holmes's forces in Arkansas, the forces closest at hand and least employed, were not under Bragg's command.[32] The inability of Bragg to draw on large numbers of troops in Arkansas was a major flaw in the Confederate command structure and would continue to be a problem for the remainder of the year.

General Bragg decided to concentrate his resources in Tennessee to force the fight back into central Tennessee towards Kentucky. On 21 July, Bragg reinforced Kirby Smith with the Army of the Mississippi, moving his headquarters to Chattanooga. Bragg left Van Dorn to defend Vicksburg and Price with his army to defend northern Mississippi. On his departure Bragg ordered Van Dorn to "consult and freely cooperate" with Price, hardly a sound command arrangement considering the distances involved.[33] Bragg's plan called for a joint maneuver into Tennessee with Price and Van Dorn conducting supporting attacks. Problems resulting from the lack of guidance provided by Bragg began immediately after his departure. Van Dorn wanted to attack due north, clearing west Tennessee and moving into Nashville. Price wanted to attack northeast from his base at Tupelo towards Corinth thereby directly supporting Bragg's offensive. Price believed he had been given specific guidance from Bragg to conduct this maneuver. As a result of the obvious disarray and in an attempt to solidify the planning, the Confederate War Department ordered Van Dorn to assume command of all forces in Mississippi. He responded that he could not accept command over Price as their concepts were too divergent. Bragg, although in overall command, did not intervene, allowing his two subordinates to work the problems out themselves.[34]

On the 13th of September, Van Dorn's army approached and threatened Corinth while Price seized Iuka.[35] The singular lack of cooperation exhibited, and the repulse of Price's army by Ord, led the Confederate Secretary of War George W. Randolph to rebuke Van Dorn. He ordered him to assume command and to make proper disposition for the defense of the Mississippi River and the advance into Tennessee.[36] It is hardly a wonder that the Confederate government felt the need to usurp its generals in the field.

Recognizing the limitations of Van Dorn and Price and the growing threat to the Mississippi, the Confederates initiated the first of a series of assignments which significantly enhanced their ability to defend Mississippi. On 30 September 1862, Randolph ordered Major General John C. Pemberton to proceed to Jackson, Mississippi, to relieve Major General Van Dorn of his district. This would enable Van Dorn to command the advance into west Tennessee and would ensure the defense of Mississippi and Louisiana east of the Mississippi River.[37] Pemberton's control over all operations was confirmed on 14 October with his nomination to lieutenant general and assignment to command of all forces operating in southwestern Tennessee.

Van Dorn's offensive from northern Mississippi into

Tennessee in support of Bragg's attacks met bitter defeat at the battle of Corinth on 3 and 4 October. Complete victory slipped through Rosecrans's fingers as he allowed Van Dorn to escape.[38] The battle of Corinth marked the turning point in the campaign in northern Mississippi. According to Grant, the campaign...

> Relieved me from further anxiety for the safety of the territory within my jurisdiction, and soon after receiving reinforcements I suggested to the general-in-chief a forward movement against Vicksburg.[39]

By the end of October, Van Dorn had successfully retreated and was fortified on the Tallahatchie River while maintaining occupation forces at Holly Springs and Grand Junction on the Mississippi Central Railroad.[40]

FOCUS ON VICKSBURG

The battle of Corinth and the retreat of Confederate forces resulted in the focus of all Union offensive campaign planning and Confederate defensive preparations to shift to the priority objective, Vicksburg. Vicksburg lay on a sharp bend in the Mississippi River on the highest bluffs in the region. Only the strongest ironclad could risk passing Vicksburg without suffering terrible damage from guns placed on the bluffs. Although Union forces controlled the river on both sides of

Vicksburg, no commercial traffic dared pass.

Pemberton set to work defending Vicksburg with his armies fortifying along the Tallahatchie in northern Mississippi and by improving the immediate defenses of the fortress. Pemberton's operational preparations were relatively easy; Vicksburg could only be approached from the river, or along the bluff leading towards Grenada.

Brigadier General Daniel Ruggles, commanding the Confederate District of Mississippi, had previously alerted the War Department to the danger of ceding the Yazoo River just north of Vicksburg. Union gunboats could navigate the river all the way to the Mississippi Central Railroad and, from the river, fan out destroying the fertile hinterland.[41] Furthermore, the Yazoo held considerable Confederate boat building facilities near Yazoo City and offered the only dry landing places for Union forces north of Vicksburg. Recognizing that under the present circumstances the Yazoo was critical to Vicksburg's defense, Pemberton initiated defensive works on the Yazoo immediately. Twenty miles up the Yazoo, at Snyder's Bluff, he positioned batteries overlooking a raft blocking the river.[42] On 24 October Pemberton sent his personal Inspector General and Adjutant, Colonel William S. Lovell, to Haynes' Bluff (just north of Snyder's Bluff's) on the Yazoo with instructions to:

> Examine the road between that place and
> Vicksburg; the condition of the obstruction of said

25

river; state the best point to establish a battery near the obstructions; number of troops;... You will make a similar inspection of Vicksburg.[43]

Lovell's report did not alleviate Pemberton's concerns. Virtually no heavy guns existed or were available on the Yazoo. The number of heavy guns at Vicksburg was not satisfactory and those that were available were oriented only on an attack from the river. Pemberton requested immediate assistance from the War Department to reinforce Vicksburg and the Yazoo with twenty siege guns from 12 to 24 pounders to strengthen the land defenses.[44] By the beginning of November, Pemberton was firmly on the defensive in northern Mississippi and was rapidly arming Vicksburg.

The initiative had passed again to Grant. Grant's attention had begun to shift towards Vicksburg in September. Butler had alerted Halleck to a menacing build up of Confederate ironclads on the Yazoo River.[45] Halleck tasked Grant with the mission to destroy the boats in a cooperative effort with Brigadier General Frederick Steele at Helena, Arkansas. This venture developed into the first serious squabble resulting from Halleck's inability to firmly establish the chain of command in the west. Steele's division belonged to Curtis, commander of the Department of Missouri. The Mississippi River divided Grant's and Curtis's department, a fundamental mistake of military art, and cooperation was required for any venture against the Yazoo. Steele's division at Helena was of no value to operations in Arkansas and its proximity to Grant made it an operational necessity to support him. Forewarned by Sherman as to the difficulties that Curtis was capable of making, Grant was compelled to meet Curtis at St. Louis to organize the effort.[46] Obtaining Curtis's cheerful cooperation was not an easy task. Grant went armed with Halleck's message empowering him to command Steele.

Grant's plan on the Yazoo was to "move on Grenada to attract attention in that direction while Steele moves across below" and he tasked Sherman to develop the details and lead the operation.[47] Grant found the right man for the job. Although the plan never came to fruition due to the Confederate assault on Corinth, the assignment of Sherman produced invaluable planning data for future operations and a man who, like Grant, would attack a problem with single minded purpose. Sherman was a visionary and a prolific writer of his military concepts. Whereas Grant created a rift before Shiloh by failing to keep Halleck informed, Sherman wrote extensively to his superiors on his strategic and operational concepts. Sherman turned his attention to the Yazoo mission and studied the terrain and various offensive operations open to Union forces.[48] On 4 October, Sherman wrote to Grant:

> This is my hobby, and I know you pardon me when I say that I am daily more and more convinced that we should hold the river absolutely and leave the interior alone. Detachments inland can always be overcome or are at great hazard, and they do not convert people. ...With the Mississippi safe we could land troops at any point, and by a quick march break the railroad.[49]

While Grant and Sherman planned their moves, to the east was developing one of the most interesting political aspects of the campaign on the Mississippi River. Major General John A. McClernand, a former Democratic congressman and division commander under Grant, had left the western army in August to recruit in his home state of Illinois. A personal friend of Lincoln's, McClernand dispatched a long letter to him on 28 September 1862 in which he emphasized the commercial necessity of clearing the Mississippi River. He described the plummeting morale in the western states from the loss in revenue and he proposed a river expedition of 60,000 men to descend the river to the mouth of the Yazoo River and to embark at the best spot to assault Vicksburg. Simultaneously, a column from the Gulf would attack overland to seize Jackson, Mississippi. McClernand offered his services to recruit the forces required and to lead the expedition. Lincoln was smitten with the plan and with the promise of large reinforcements recruited by McClernand. Lincoln was also much impressed with McClernand. On 1 October 1862 President Lincoln had a discussion with newly appointed Rear Admiral David Porter in which Lincoln asked him who would be best to command this operation. Porter replied that either Grant or Sherman should command whereupon Lincoln responded that "I have in mind a better general than either of them; that is McClernand, an old and intimate friend of mine."[51]

Lincoln's orders to McClernand were transmitted through Secretary of War Stanton bypassing Halleck completely, a fact that Halleck would use to his advantage in dealing with McClernand later in the year. On 21 October, Stanton ordered McClernand to proceed to Indiana, Illinois, and Iowa to organize troops and forward them to Memphis or Cairo as directed by the General-in-Chief:

> To the end that, when a sufficient force not required by the operations of General Grant's command shall be raised, an expedition may be organized under General McClernand's command against Vicksburg and to clear the Mississippi River and open navigation to New Orleans.[52]

On 24 October, Halleck made a major departmental reorganization in the west by relieving Major General Don Carlos Buell as commander of the Department of the Ohio and replacing him with Major General Rosecrans. Halleck ordered

Grant to assume command of the Department of the Tennessee with the field army of the department designated as the XIIIth Army Corps (See Appendix). The more popular name that would develop for this corps was the Army of the Tennessee.[53]

With reinforcements filtering into Memphis in late October, Grant initiated the first stage of his offensive efforts. Sherman had continued to press Grant for a strike oh the Yazoo and Mississippi Central Railroads while Pemberton's forces were north of the Tallahatchie.[54]

Grant's aide, Colonel William S. Hillyer wrote Sherman on 29 October that since Curtis continually failed to cooperate in any way, "the general has abandoned all idea of the expedition".[55] Grant was also beginning to read newspaper accounts of a river expedition forming under McClernand and Curtis, and no doubt attributed Curtis's intransigence to this expedition.[56] Grant began a movement of XIIIth Army Corps out of LaGrange on 2 November and sent a dispatch to Halleck:

> I have commenced a movement on Grand Junction, with three divisions from Corinth and two from Bolivar... If found practicable; I will go to Holly Springs, and maybe, Gienada...[57]

By 8 November, Grant had taken Grand Junction and LaGrange.

During the period 3 November to 10 November, Grant saw his first concrete evidence of McClernand's expedition in a series of messages from Halleck. The first on 3 November reported that "I hope for an active campaign on the Mississippi this fall. A large force will ascend the river from New Orleans."[58] On 10 November Halleck told Grant that "Memphis will be made the depot of a joint military and naval expedition on Vicksburg."[59] Confused about these cryptic messages, and certainly aware of the rumors of McClernand's adventures, Grant asked "am I to understand that I lie still here while an expedition is fitted out from Memphis or do you want me to push as far south as possible?"[60] Halleck found a loophole that Secretary Stanton had consciously or unconsciously placed in the last line of McClernand's original orders. The orders stipulated that the forces would remain subject to Halleck's orders and that the forces available for the expedition were contingent upon Grant's own force requirements. Halleck wired to Grant on 11 November: "You have command of all troops sent to your department, and have permission to fight the enemy where you please."[61] Halleck, like Grant, was not impressed with McClernand as a professional soldier. Although brave in battle, both were of the same opinion as Grant voiced, "I did not think the general selected had either the experience or the qualifications to fit him for so important a position."[62]

By 9 November the threat from the north caused Pemberton to order Van Dorn to evacuate positions north of the

Tallahatchie River and occupy defensive positions south of the river." The obvious threat developing in northern Mississippi led Pemberton to coordinate and lay the groundwork with the Confederate War Department for a new defensive strategy for his department.

On 18 November, Pemberton wired Secretary of War Randolph requesting General Bragg to move to threaten the rear of Grant's forces and requested immediate reinforcements. The next day the War Department placed Pemberton officially under Bragg's command and also directed Holmes at Little Rock, Arkansas, to send 10,000 men to Vicksburg.[65] Bragg responded appropriately; Holmes did not. Bragg outlined a plan on 21 November to "send a cavalry force under Forrest to create a diversion by assailing their rear and communications in west Tennessee."[66] Holmes dithered and replied that he couia not get to Vicksburg in less than two weeks, and by that time Union forces from Helena would be threatening his own department.[67]

While Pemberton scrambled to shore up his defenses in Mississippi, the Confederate government was in the throes of an intense debate over the prosecution of the western war. On 12 November, General Joseph E. Johnston reported fit for duty after recovering from wounds received in Virginia. Johnston was told by Secretary Randolph that he would go west to command. Johnston suggested to Randolph that the best strategy in the west was to unite all the armies, thereby outnumbering the Union for the first time. This united army would first destroy the threat in Mississippi and then turn and overwhelm Rosecrans in Tennessee. Coincidentally, this was Randolph's own position on the appropriate strategy. He showed Johnston a letter which President Davis had countermanded which would have brought Holmes's army over the Mississippi River into Pemberton's command. Davis would not relinquish Arkansas although the Union threat was minimal and the strategic value slight. Randolph retired several days later in protest.[68]

On 24 November, Johnston was formally assigned the overall command of the departments of Generals Bragg, Smith, and Pemberton (See Appendix). Responding to these orders, Johnston wrote the Secretary of War of the necessity of moving Holmes over the Mississippi, but as Johnston later wrote "This suggestion was not adopted, nor noticed."[69] The territorial defense policy Davis cherished was reinforced even though the loss of Arkansas would have been comparatively insignificant. The disagreement over policy, added to a long standing feud between Johnston and Davis sparked by an earlier promotion slight, did not bode well for future Confederate command harmony.

Union naval efforts on the Mississippi River were increased in October and November with the new mission assigned to the flotilla to prepare to support McClernand's river expedition. In October, Rear Admiral David D. Porter received orders to take command of the Mississippi Squadron and prepare to support McClernand's river expedition. In October, Rear Admiral David D. Porter received orders to take command of the Mississippi Squadron and prepare it for action against Vicksburg. By 29 October Porter reported to Secretary of the Navy Gideon Welles "I am ready to move on Vicksburg."[70] By mid November Porter was caught squarely in the middle of the muddled ground forces command problem. Through the Secretary of the Navy he was receiving preparatory guidance for the McClernand expedition. From the west, he was continually asked to support Curtis's forces at Helena. Additionally, Grant requested support and assistance in his offensive operations. Porter's successful juggling of these requirements attests to his skill as a commander.

On 16 November Sherman advised Porter of possible Confederate fortifications at the mouth of the Yazoo River which he had become aware of during his raid planning in October. Sherman offered Porter, who readily accepted, all the maps and planning figures that he had prepared. Porter had a deep affinity for Sherman and Grant, believing them to be in his class of professional soldiers, and always expended extra effort to help them. Additionally, he knew that no matter who commanded the river expedition those batteries had to be eliminated. On 21 November Porter dispatched a naval expedition to take out the batteries and to make a landing assessment. On 29 November the gunboats <u>Marmora</u> and <u>Signal</u> traversed the Yazoo finding fortifications at Drumgould's Bluff, approximately twenty miles upriver. Drumgould's Bluff was the center bluff in a chain of three bluffs on which the Confederates had based their defense. South of Drumgould's Bluff was Snyder's Bluff and to the north was Haynes' Bluff. For purposes of identification, the proximity of Snyder's Bluff and Drumgould's Bluff to each other have caused the names to be used interchangeably in battle planning. The naval officers on the gunboats found the works were too extensive to destroy and returned to stations on the Mississippi River.[71]

Success in his overland campaign and the clear go ahead from Halleck spurred Grant to call Sherman with two divisions out of Memphis. Grant's combined army pressed forward at the Tallahatchie while a force from Brigadier General Steele's command at Helena crossed the Mississippi, threatening Pemberton's left flank and rear.

By 30 November Pemberton felt besieged. Facing him

was the overwhelming majority of Grant's army. On his flank had appeared the force from Helena. Spies had warned him of a river expedition forming at Memphis. Pemberton pleaded with Davis for reinforcements from Holmes and cooperation from Bragg.[72] Bragg immediately responded by sending a strong brigade under Brigadier General John C. Vaughn to reinforce Pemberton.[73] Fearing that Steele's forces would outflank his defenses and with Grant's cavalry in control of key crossing points on the Tallahatchie, Pemberton began a withdrawal on 30 November, reestablishing his defensive line at the Yalabusha by 5 December.[74]

During the final two weeks in November Grant came to realize that McClernand's expedition was going to occur, like it or not. On 24 November Porter warned Sherman that McClernand would be ready to join in the attack on Vicksburg in three weeks.[75] Halleck could no longer passively fail to support the buildup and planning for McClernand, advising Grant of his plan for a supporting movement from New Orleans and asked him on 23 November how many men he could have available to send on the river expedition under McClernand.[76] Grant realized that his force was slipping out of his hands. Halleck, however, sought to allow Grant the fullest latitude possible. Throughout November, McClernand requested orders from Stanton to move forward from Illincis to command the expedition.[77] The orders were not forthcoming. Halleck was delaying as long as possible, in part feigning ignorance of the operation but mostly from exasperation with:

> how difficult it is to resist politiical wire pulling in military appointments. Every governor, Senator, and Member of Congress has his pet generals to be provided with separate and independent commands.[78]

Convinced of the inevitable and "desiring to have a competent commander in charge," Grant reoriented his campaign from a land operation to focus on an amphibious operation under a commander of his choice.[79] On 4 December 1862, even in the face of an obvious Confederate stampede south, Grant halted his drive in order to shift forces and the commander of his choice, Sherman, to Memphis. The necessity for haste was essential in order to embark before McClernand could arrive. The premature halt of Grant's offensive was to prove to be as critical to the Confederates as Halleck's timidity at Corinth. Again, the Confederates had been given a respite at a difficult moment.

By 4 December 1862 when Grant shifted his campaign plan to the amphibious operation, eventually to be known as the Chickasaw Bayou campaign, Union and Confederate strategic activities had been well developed. The implications of the strategic developments directly affected the campaigns to seize control of the Mississippi River. In the north the singular lack of central direction and unity of command following Halleck's departure to Washington created the conditions under which the campaign was initiated and eventually failed. Without a single and clearly designated commander in the west, President Lincoln and his Secretary of War were able to insert a separate army under McClernand into Grant's area of operations. This army intended to draw significant resources from Grant's efforts and clearly challenged Grant's authority. Recognizing the threat imposed by this venture, Halleck and Grant actively maneuvered to circumvent this plan. The sad outcome of the presidential interference was that it caused Grant to stop a successful overland offensive and form his own river expedition.

Of lesser importance yet a constantly aggravating shortcoming resulting from the lack of unity of command were the habitual failures of adjacent commanders to support Grant. Halleck promised support for Grant from New Orleans and from Rosecrans to pin Confederate reserves. Grant, however, had no authority over those forces. Those forces in New Orleans would be critical to any effort against Vicksburg, yet Grant had to communicate through Washington for any cooperation. Finally, Grant's department was divided by the Mississippi River from Curtis's Department of the Missouri.

Those forces were of little value in Arkansas and were in excellent pr,sition to support Grant. Curtis habitually failed to support any activities on the Mississippi without direct intervention from Halleck.

The Confederates cemented the most important ingredients in their strategic plans in the short period before the campaign. The initial assignment of Pemberton Shored up defenses in Mississippi and in particular the defense of Vicksburg. The assignment of Johnston unified the Confederate efforts in the theater and would prove crucial during the campaign. A fatal flaw was built into the chain of command that would manifest itself much later, although fortunately not for the Confederates at Chickasaw Bayou. Just over the Mississippi were 20,000 troops conducting a Davis-inspired territorial defense of Arkansas. They were not under Johnston's control because Davis knew that Johnston would abandon Arkansas to defend the critical Mississippi valley.

Regardless of the circumstances under which Grant found himself in the first days of December, he saw only prospects for success in his future operations. Grant knew his forces significantly outnumbered Pemberton's. In every engagement he had been victorious and the influx of reinforcements into Memphis bolstered his confidence in a river operation. Grant was a commander who liked to use circumstances to his advantage as they presented themselves. Unlike Sherman, Grant did not spend a great deal of time developing long range plans, preferring to adjust to the conditions developed by battle. In this framework, and knowing that Sherman and Porter had already done an in depth study of the Yazoo River, Grant felt no hesitation shifting to a river offensive.

ENDNOTES

1. Abraham Lincoln's Presidential General War Order, 27 Jan 1862, <u>The Collected Works of Abraham Lincoln</u> ed. Roy P. Basler, 8 vols. (New Brunswick: Rutgers University Press, 1953) 5: 111.

2. Archer Jones, <u>Confederate Strategy from Shiloh to Vicksburg</u> (Baton Rouge: Louisiana University Press, 1961), 5.

3. Ibid., 5 & 6.

4. Ibid., 6.

5. Report of MG John A. McClernand, 28 Sept 1862, <u>The War Union and Confederate Armies</u> 128 vols. (Washington: Government Printing Office, 1880-1901) Series I, Vol. XVII, Part 2: 849. (Cited hereafter as <u>OR</u>)

6. Jones,   6.

7. Ibid.

8. Ibid., 7.

9. Ibid., 7 & 27.

10. Ibid., 8.

11. Ibid., 21.

12. Ibid., 19.

13. Ibid., 26.

14. Ibid., 25.

15. William T. Sherman, <u>Memoirs of General W.T. Sherman</u> (New York: The Library of America, 1990), 302.

16. Jones, 51 & 52.

17. Earl S. Miers, The Web of Victory (New York: Alfred A. Knopf, 1955) , 12, 14-17.

18. James L. McDonough, Shiloh - in Hell before Night (Knoxville: The University of Tennessee Press, 1977), 7.

19. Ibid., 9.

20. Miers, 19, 20.

21. Jones, 57.

22. Sherman, 274, 275.

23. Stephen D. Lee, "The Campaign of General Grant and Sherman against Vicksburg in December 1862 and January 1st and 2d, 1863, known as the 'Chickasaw Bayou Campaign' " in Publications of the Mississippi Historical Society, ed. Franklin L. Riley, (Oxford, Mississippi: Harrisburg Publishing Co., 1902) IV: 15,16.

24. OR, Series I, Vol. XVII, Part 2, 26.

25. Ibid., 43.

26. Ibid., 97.

27. Ibid.

28. U.S. Grant, The Personal Memoirs of U.S. Grant (New York: The World Publishing Co., 1952), 204 and OR, Series I, Vol. XVII, Part 1, 4.

29. Grant, 210.

30. Jones, 61.

31. <u>OR</u>, Series I, Vol. XVII, Part 1, 1 & 2.

32. Jones, 72.

33. Ibid., 74.

34. Ibid., 78.

35. Sherman, 281.

36. Jones, 79.

37. <u>OR</u>, Series I, Vol. XVII, Part 2, 716.

38. Grant, 216-217.

39. Ibid., 218.

40. Ibid., 210.

41. <u>OR</u>, Series I, Vol. XVII, Part 2, 722.

42. Ibid., 724.

43. Ibid., 736.

44. Ibid., 749.

45. <u>OR</u>, Series I, Vol. XVII, Part 2, 225.

46. Ibid., 179, 234-235.

47. Ibid., 240-241.

48. Ibid., 244-245.

49. Ibid., 260.

50. Ibid., 849.

51. David D. Porter, <u>Incidents and Anecdotes of the Civil War</u> (New York: D. Appleton and Co., 1891), 122.

52 <u>OR</u>, Series, Series I, Vol. XVII, Part 2, 282.

53. Edwin C. Bearss, <u>The Campaign For Vicksburg</u> 3 Vols.

(Dayton, OH: Morningside House, Inc., 1985), 21-22.

54. <u>OR</u>, Series I, Vol. XVII, Part 2, 285.

55. Ibid., 307.

56. Ibid., 220.

57. Grant, 220.

58. <u>OR</u>, Series I, Vol. XVII, Part 1, 467.

59. Ibid., 468.

60. Ibid.,469.

61. Ibid.

62. Grant, 222.

63. Ibid.

64. <u>OR,</u> Series I, Vol. XVII, Part 2,751.

65. Ibid., 752-753.

66. Ibid., 755.

67. Ibid., 757.

68. Joseph E. Johnston, <u>Narrative of Military Operations during the Civil War</u> (Bloomington: Indiana University Press, 1959), 147-149.

69. Ibid., 150.

70. The War of Rebellion: A Compilation of the Official Records of the Union and Confederate Navies, 31 vols. (Washington: Government Printing Office, Series I, Vol. XXIII: 458. (Cited hereafter as <u>ORN</u>).

71. Ibid., 500.

72. <u>OR</u>, Series I, Vol. XVII, Part 2, 767.

73. Ibid., 769.

74. Ibid., 778.

75. ORN, Series I, Vol. XXIII, 500.

76. <u>OR</u>, Series I, Vol. XVII, Part I, 471.

77. <u>OR</u>, Series I, Vol. XVII, Part 2, 371.

78. Herman Hattaway and Archer Jones, <u>How the North Won</u> (Chicago: University of Illinois Press, 1983), 309 - 310.

79. Grant, 223.

CHAPTER TWO OPERATIONAL PLANS
4 DECEMBER-25 DECEMBER 1862

See what a lot of land these fellows hold, of which Vicksburg is the key. ...Let us get Vicksburg and all that country is ours. The war can never be brought to a close until that key is in our pocket.
Abraham Lincoln, October 1862[1]

GRANT'S OPERATIONAL PLANNING

In a series of messages to Halleck on 4 and 5 December, Grant outlined his current status and problems and proposed his new campaign plan. On 4 December Grant asked Halleck for guidance as to how far south he should move in his current operations. He tentatively recommended a plan to move a force from Memphis and Helena against Vicksburg. On 5 December Grant reinforced the necessity to cancel his current overland operations and move down river due to the impassability of the roads and the danger of having to leave the railroad at Grenada in an overland campaign. He specifically identified Sherman as the probable commander of the amphibious force and requested command of Curtis's troops at Helena. With these forces under his command he promised to secure Vicksburg and the state of Mississippi.[2]

Halleck, concerned since his days as western commander about projecting an army overland into Mississippi and happy to foil the McClernand expedition, readily assented. Halleck responded on the 5th ordering Grant to disable the Mobile road, disable the others to Grenada, and not to hold the area south of the Tallahatchie River. Halleck directed that the:

> Troops for Vicksburg should be back to Memphis by the 20th. If possible collect at that place, for that purpose, as many as 25,000. More will be added from Helena, etc. Your main object will be to hold the line from Memphis to Corinth with as small a force as possible, while the largest number is thrown upon Vicksburg with the gunboats.[3]

On 7 December Halleck alerted Grant that he could employ all of Curtis's troops in Helena and in Mississippi. He told Grant that Brigadier General Robert Allen, Chief Quartermaster at St. Louis, would provide steamers, and he authorized coordination with Rear Admiral Porter for gunboat assistance.[4] At this point in the war the navy controlled the gunboats and rams, the army quartermaster service controlled river boats. Oddly, Halleck also indicated that the seizure of Grenada might change Grant's plans for Vicksburg. This vacillation from previous guidance and his next statement to "Move your troops as best you deem necessary" may have been either supreme confidence in Grant or self protection in the event of failure.

In any event, by 8 December Grant was confident in his ability to hold in north central Mississippi and detach suitable forces to move down the river. Grant initiated his new campaign with a series of directives to subordinates and requests for support to Curtis and Porter. Grant designated Sherman to be the commander of the Right Wing, Thirteenth Army Corps and gave him the major burden of responsibility (See Appendix). Grant directed him in a written order to proceed immediately with one division to Memphis. At Memphis Sherman was to organize all forces there, as well as Curtis's forces east of the Mississippi River, into brigades and divisions. Once organized, he was to move down river to the vicinity of Vicksburg with the support of the gunboat fleet under Admiral Porter. At Vicksburg he was directed by Grant to "proceed to the reduction of that place in such a manner as you dictate" and Grant promised to "cooperate with you in such a manner as the movements of the enemy will make necessary."[5]

This last line does not make clear Grant's intent and would become a source of some controversy. Grant did make his point clear orally to Sherman in a meeting at Oxford on 7 December and hints at it in a communication to Halleck on 8 December. Whether he communicated his intent properly in writing is a point debated by historians, but to Sherman there was no doubt. In the meeting Grant specified that Sherman would land at a suitable point on the Yazoo River and capture

Vicksburg from the rear. Grant with the remaining troops from the Department of Tennessee would constitute the main body of the Thirteenth Army Corps and would maneuver his troops to prevent Pemberton from reinforcing Vicksburg. If Pemberton retreated south, Grant would follow and link up with Sherman at the Yazoo or Vicksburg. Grant also told him that Halleck had promised that Major General Nathanial P. Banks in New Orleans would support by working his way up river while Sherman moved down.[6] Grant gave additional instructions to Sherman to cut the Mississippi Central Railroad and the Southern Railroad, the major rail line running east and west out of Vicksburg.[7] Grant's intent was clear. He would not abandon the railroad north of the Yalabusha or push southward unless Pemberton retreated. In this event he intended to "hold the road to Grenada on the Yalabusha and cut loose from there, expecting to establish a new base of supplies on the Yazoo, or at Vicksburg itself."[8] Grant advised Sherman that another expedition was expected from New Orleans under Major General Nathanial Banks. Without any control over this force, Grant did not seem to put much faith in its arrival. In a message to Halleck, Grant specified how he planned to hold Pemberton's army in the interior. He intended to use his large force of cavalry "to show themselves at different points on the Tallahatchie and Yalabusha, and where an opportunity occurs make a real attack."[9]

On 8 December, Grant sent a message to Steele at Helena, Arkansas, advising Steele that his force currently on the east side of the Mississippi was no longer under Curtis but was attached to the Thirteenth Army Corps. Grant outlined his scheme of maneuver and requested a status report of the forces available.[10] Steele was a fighter with no respect for Curtis. Grant knew that in Steele, a West Point classmate, he had an ally and purposely bypassed Curtis in the coordination.

Halleck continued to worry and vacillate in his guidance indicating that he may well not have understood the military situation in the west. On 9 December, fearful of an offensive by Bragg, he telegraphed Grant not to endanger West Tennessee by using too many troops on the river expedition. Again, this was very different guidance from what he had originally given to Grant just days before. In this communication the spector of McClernand loomed again with the comment that "The president may insist upon designating a separate commander; if not, assign such officers as you deem best."[11] Halleck knew only too well that McClernand was this "separate commander" and that the decision had been made; he was trying to alarm and thus hurry Grant. Halleck's insinuations achieved his purpose. Grant admitted in his memoirs that the rumors, newspaper accounts, and Halleck's messages caused him great concern and he rushed Sherman back to Memphis in order to prevent McClernand's assumption of command. The haste in which the campaign was mounted was to become a source of criticism in later years and pointed to as one of the reasons for failure at Chickasaw Bayou.

SHERMAN'S OPERATIONAL PLANNING AND PREPARATIONS

Sherman was well prepared to initiate the new campaign. His previous experience in planning the mission to destroy Confederate gunboats on the Yazoo River and his own personal study of river operations to take Vicksburg were essential to fast planning and preparation. Sherman immediately dispatched Colonel Benjamin H. Grierson with his cavalry to Helena to take Grant's message notifying Steele of the plan. Sherman then moved to College Hill, Mississippi, and selected Brigadier General Morgan L. Smith's Second division to accompany him to Memphis, leaving his First and Third Divisions with the main body of the Thirteenth Corps. Also on 8 December Sherman initiated direct coordination with Rear Admiral Porter at Cairo, Illinois, describing his tentative plans of operation and gunboat requirements. With the forces assigned, Sherman proposed to move down river, cut the road from Monroe, Louisiana, to Jackson, Mississippi (the Southern

Railroad), and then appear on the Yazoo to threaten the Mississippi Central Railroad. Sherman said that these movements would have to be done be re the winter rains and that necessitated extreme haste and movement out of Memphis by 20 December. In concluding his message, Sherman asked Porter to meet him in Memphis to coordinate the effort.[13]

Sherman arrived back in Memphis on 12 December finding two newly arrived divisions commanded by Brigadier General Andrew J. Smith and Brigadier General George W. Morgan. These divisions were composed of a small number of veteran regiments heavily attrited by this stage of the war. In addition, a large number of McClernand's recently recruited midwestern regiments were encamped awaiting McClernand's arrival.[14] Sherman's immediate task was the reorganization of his ground forces (See Appendix). He quickly allocated the regiments to each of the three Memphis divisions and organized his regiments into brigades. The First Division, commanded by Brigadier General A.J. Smith, was composed of three brigades with twelve infantry regiments with about 7,350 men. The Second Division, commanded by Brigadier General Morgan L. Smith, was composed of two brigades with ten infantry regiments with about 6,000 men. The Third Division under George W. Morgan was composed of three brigades with ten infantry regiments with about 6,700 men. Sherman's artillery consisted of eight batteries with forty guns and four 30 pounder rifled siege guns.[15]

Sherman also learned that Steele no longer commanded the forces at Helena and that Curtis had placed Brigadier General Willis A. Gorman in command. Anticipating problems and believing that Grierson had failed to get to Helena, Sherman sent an aide to ensure that Gorman understood the requirement for 12,000 infantry and 2,000 cavalry.

Sherman's message indicated that he expected from Gorman three strong brigades of at least 10,000 infantry under Steele's command which Sherman planned to designate as the Fourth Division, Right Wing, Thirteenth Army Corps. Sherman also advised Gorman that Grant wanted 2,000 cavalry posted on the east side of the Mississippi at the Tallahatchie and one regiment of infantry to be stationed at Friars Point, Mississippi. Sherman anticipated using Friars Point as the first rendezvous on the river and its security was essential.[18] To Grant and Halleck he reported that all preparations were going as desired and he anticipated embarking on the 18th of December with 20,523 soldiers from Memphis and about 12,000 more men from Helena, Arkansas.[17]

Sherman had correctly anticipated that the coordination for Steele's division would not be easy and Gorman's response elicited a spate of messages between Grant, Sherman, Curtis,

Gorman and Steele. Gorman told Sherman and Grant that he could provide only 5,000 infantry and 2,000 cavalry unless ordered by Curtis to do otherwise.[18] Coincidentally, just the day before, Curtis had asked Halleck for command of the river expedition, clearly displaying the basis for his poor support of Grant's requests. In response, Halleck had deftly claimed that Lincoln had in mind another commander, a commander whose identity had "not been communicated to me." Halleck also told him that until otherwise told, that commander would be the senior officer present; that officer was clearly Grant. Sherman was incensed with Gorman's response and telegraphed Curtis on 13 December telling him flatly that 12,000 troops were required and that he wanted those troops released right away.[19] Steele added fuel to the fire with a message that same day to Sherman describing Curtis's "damned rascality" and openly accused his superior of hindering the effort to seize Vicksburg.

By 15 December Grant advised Sherman to take whatever measures were necessary to get all the available troops from Helena. Grant told Sherman to take command of the whole garrison if necessary, implying that the use of force was authorized.[21] As it turned out, with more coaxing from Halleck and Sherman, Curtis directed that the appropriate force be provided.

Meanwhile, at Cairo, Illinois, Union quartermasters

toiled diligently to amass river boat transportation for 30,000 soldiers. Chief Quartermaster Allen was given less than ten days to deliver the boats. Allen told the army field commanders they would have to burn wood from the sides of the river because of the lack of coal but that they would get the boats in time.[22]

PORTER'S OPERATIONS

Rear Admiral Porter's appointment to the command of the Mississippi Squadron in October 1862 came as a result of the transfer of that squadron from the War Department to the Navy. The squadron consisted primarily of ironclad gunboats. In addition to Porter's fleet were the independent transport river boats under Brigadier General Allen, and the Ram Fleet under Colonel Charles R. Ellet, both under War Department control. The Ram Fleet soon became a Navy responsibility, but would remain under an army officer due to the habitual employment of ground forces from these boats.[23]

In preparation for the McClernand expedition, Porter had established a small flotilla of gunboats and rams at the mouth of the Yazoo River under the command of Captain Henry Walke. Its mission was to provide intelligence on enemy activities, to gradually clear the Yazoo channel of torpedoes, and to hold the Yazoo River at all costs.[24]

The movement of this force down river in November had been one of the sparks that caused Pemberton to fall behind the Yalabusha, believing that the rumored river invasion was occurring. With the prolonged stay of Walke's force in the vicinity of the Yazoo River, Confederate concern waned.

On 12 December the navy suffered its only serious loss on the river during the campaign. Captain Walke had ordered two gunboats, the Marmora and Signal, to recon the river. Twenty miles up they found a large number of torpedoes just short of an excellent landing spot near Snyder's Bluff. Walke ordered Captain E.W. Sutherland with four gunboats: the Marmora, Signal, Cairo, and Pittsburg; and the ram Queen of the West, to remove the torpedoes. Under a brisk fire from the fortifications on the bluff, the force maneuvered in the center channel of the Yazoo to remove the command detonated torpedoes. In the process, the gunboat Cairo hit a torpedo, or one was detonated from the shore against it, and sank. The force returned to the Mississippi reporting the loss to Porter. In his report Captain Walke concluded that a land force with the gunboats would be required to clear that portion of the river near Snyder's Bluff and that the Yazoo River was well sown with obstacles.[25]

Following receipt of Sherman's message of 8 December, Porter dispatched every available gunboat and ram from Cairo to Memphis. His only problem was outfitting crews for the light draft vessels. These boats would be crucial to ferrying supplies up the Yazoo River or any of the small tributaries to Grant's force, should that be necessary. In any event Porter saw little action for the navy in the campaign, recognizing that once ashore the gunboats could do little to support the attacks inland.[26] Whether his navy would get glory in the coming operations was of no concern to Porter. Porter would do anything for his two revered army compatriots. Having completed the necessary arrangements to move his boats, Porter departed Cairo, Illinois, on 13 December to meet with Sherman and coordinate the river offensive. Weighing heavily on Porter's mind was the loss of a prized gunboat, and the necessity to clear the Yazoo before heavily laden troop transports were put in jeopardy.

McCLERNAND

McClernand's recruitment efforts were completed by the end of November. Anxiously awaiting the call to go forward to command the expedition, McClernand wrote Lincoln and Stanton on 12 December for his orders. Stanton wired back on 15 December that "I had supposed that you had received your orders from the General-in-Chief. I will see him and have the matter attended to without delay." If Stanton did approach

Halleck, no orders resulted and Halleck continued to delay.[27] By the 17th, McClernand suspected foul play. In a simple message to Lincoln and Stanton he stated, "I believe I have been superseded." Stanton replied that "It surprises me, but I will ascertain and let you know immediately."[28] McClernand's communication forced Halleck to act. Halleck again responded in a characteristically deliberate fashion hoping that the expedition had already departed. On 18 December he telegraphed Grant that he must reorganize his department into four army corps. The corps were allocated with Major General J.A. McClernand commanding the Thirteenth Corps, Major General W.T. Sherman the Fifteenth, Major General S.A. Hurlbut the Sixteenth, and Major General J.B. McPherson the Seventeenth. He directed further that:

> It is the wish of the President that General McClernand's Corps shall constitute a part of the river expedition and that he shall have the immediate command under your direction.[29]

In his own communications with McClernand, Stanton sought to dispell McClernand's concern describing Grant's operations as merely efforts to organize the troops in preparation for his arrival. Regardless of Stanton's assurances, the scope of McClernand's command had been drastically reduced by his subordination to Grant, a fact that must have accelerated McClernand's anxiety.[30]

With Halleck's new orders, Grant had no choice but to initiate the handover of the amphibious wing to McClernand. On the 18th Grant sent his new instructions to McClernand and Sherman. Grant directed that McClernand's corps would be comprised of Morgan's and A.J. Smith's divisions. The divisions of Steele and M.L. Smith would be in Sherman's corps which would accompany McClernand down river. To McClernand he said "I hope you will find all preliminary preparation completed on your arrival and the expedition ready to move."[31] Grant really hoped that the expedition would already be moving before McClernand got the message.[32] Halleck also continued to delay McClernand's assumption of command. Although he had issued appropriate orders for organizational purposes, by 18 December he had still failed to issue the necessary orders to McClernand freeing him from his recruiting duties to move to his new command. Unknown to Grant, Confederate activities were also to assist Grant in his efforts to prevent McClernand's assumption of command.

CONFEDERATE OPERATIONS

General Joseph Johnston arrived at Chattanooga on 3 December following a difficult journey involving three train accidents. On arrival, Johnston received a telegram from Adjutant General Samuel Cooper at the War Department telling him of Pemberton's withdrawal to the Yalabusha and that Holmes had been ordered to reinforce. Cooper urged Johnston to send reinforcements from Bragg's army. He immediately wrote back to Cooper reiterating his desire for Holmes to support in Mississippi without the use of Bragg's forces.

Alarmed at the situation developing in northern Mississippi and desiring to establish his authority, Johnston curtly telegraphed Pemberton to "Let me know by express which way you are moving and what your plans are... I am without the necessary information. Give it."[33] Visiting Bragg's headquarters on 5 December, Johnston urged him to throw his cavalry on Grant's rear and cut communications.[34] Having already committed himself to this plan in November, Bragg readily accepted the mission though it certainty diverted even more resources from his army.

The grave situation in Mississippi and the dispute over operational plans as evidenced by Johnston's continued arguments with the War Department lead President Davis to visit the Western Theater in December. Arriving in Chattanooga on 10 December, Davis intended to try to raise civilian and military morale and at the same time settle some of the military issues.[35] In their first meeting, conducted at Bragg's headquarters at Murfreesboro, Johnston again presented his plan to rely on reinforcements from Holmes without important reinforcement from Bragg. Davis was not satisfied with this concept, vetoed it, and directed that Bragg transfer 9,000 infantry and artillery to add to Vaughn's East Tennessee Brigade already sent to Pemberton. Returning to Chattanooga, Davis personally directed which troops would be ordered to Mississippi. Under his orders, Major General Carter L. Stevenson's division, augmented by an additional brigade, were to move without delay to Jackson, Mississippi.[36] The first two brigades departed on 18 December and were forced by the loss of the Memphis-Charleston Railroad to travel circuitously through Georgia and Alabama to get to Mississippi. The remaining two brigades took three weeks in transit and were never a factor in the emerging campaign.[37]

While Johnston and Davis wrangled with the larger operational issues, Pemberton worked to shore up his Mississippi defenses. By 7 December, Pemberton was firmly positioned behind the Yalabusha River receiving very light Union pressure. Redesignating his northern forces as the First and Second Corps commanded by Van Dorn and Price respectively, Pemberton turned his attention to Vicksburg's defensive plans (See Appendix).[38] Not all the artillery Pemberton requested had arrived, but what was available was used to reinforce the vulnerable Yazoo. At Snyder's Bluff, the raft Pemberton had ordered was finished and was invulnerable to boats as long as no troops were landed to destroy it. To provide protection against that possibility Pemberton placed a light eight inch gun, a heavy eight inch gun, a twenty four pounder, a smooth bore thirty two pounder, a rifled thirty two pounder, two heavy twelve pounders, two seige twenty four pounders and light artillery on the bluff. Snyder's Bluff was now a fortress. Vaughn's East Tennesseans had arrived in Jackson on 11 December and Pemberton held them as reserves for Major General Martin L. Smith, commanding at Vicksburg.[39] Pemberton's available forces in mid December consisted of 21,000 at the Yalabusha, 6,000 at Vicksburg, and 3,000 reinforcements from Bragg.[40] No reinforcements arrived from Holmes's department despite direct orders from the War Department.

In early December Pemberton had received a letter from Lieutenant Colonel John S. Griffith, commander of the Texas Cavalry Brigade, outlining a plan for a bold cavalry raid into Grant's rear. Having already initiated a request for a strategic cavalry raid from Bragg's army, Pemberton called Griffith into a private conference to discuss the plan. Griffith recommended:

> If you will fit up a cavalry expedition, comprising three or four thousand men, and give us Major General Earl Van Dorn....we will penetrate to the rear of the enemy, capture Holly Springs, Memphis, and other points, and perhaps, force him to retreat to Coffeeville.[41]

Pemberton liked the plan and assigned Van Dorn three brigades of cavalry to execute it. This new command began to assemble at Grenada on 12 December and was composed of Colonel Griffith's Texas Brigade, Colonel William H. Jackson's Tennessee Brigade, and Colonel William McCullough's Missouri and Mississippi Brigade. On 15 December Van Dorn, at the head of this cavalry force, left Grenada and crossed the Yalabusha River beginning a flanking movement to the northeast, a maneuver shortly to have monumental consequences to the Union campaign.

On 17 December Johnston pressed Bragg to mount his cavalry raid as Pemberton feared Union forces were trying to flank him in eastern Mississippi. [42] Unknown to Johnston, Bragg had already initiated the cavalry mission. Brigadier General Nathan Bedford Forrest, the most feared and respected of Confederate cavalry leaders, had crossed the Tennessee River with his brigade of cavalry on the 15th. By the 18th, his force was beginning to assault Jackson, Tennessee, well in Grant's rear and on his only supply line.[43]

President Davis and General Johnston embarked on a tour of Alabama and Mississippi arriving in Jackson, Mississippi, on 17 December. From Jackson, Davis visited Pemberton and his army at Grenada and traveled to Vicksburg to tour the defense works. Johnston tried repeatedly to influence Davis to allow him to fight a campaign using the massed armies of Holmes and Pemberton, always to no avail. Frustrated, Johnston asked to be assigned elsewhere. He believed that the armies of Bragg and Pemberton were too far apart, had different objectives, and opposed enemies with different objectives; therefore, one general could not control them. Johnston felt that defending Vicksburg as a fortress was not the way to defeat the Union army. Rather, the combined armies of Holmes and Pemberton should break free of the city, and maneuver to defeat Grant's army. Davis did not agree and did nothing to change the defensive plans for the Mississippi Valley.[44]

From Johnston's point of view very little came out of Davis's visit; the possible exception being that for the present their relationship was cordial. From Pemberton's point of view some very satisfactory decisions had been made. Although Davis let Holmes off the hook for reinforcements, Davis had energized significant reinforcements from Bragg's army. Davis's visit also enabled Pemberton to obtain the needed support for additional artillery which Davis ordered on his behalf on 23 December. By the 18th the Confederates were well advanced in their defensive maneuvers. Reinforcements had arrived or were filtering in to support Vicksburg, the defenses on the Yalabusha were firm, and two cavalry raids were in progress.

SHERMAN'S FINAL PREPARATIONS

In the final days before the Right Wing, Thirteenth Army Corps was to embark, Sherman made final preparations for his ground forces and coordinated the use of naval assets with Rear Admiral Porter. To his ground forces, Sherman designated the First Division to occupy habitually the army's right in the attack or the advance in movement. The Second Division would occupy the center and the Third Division would occupy the left. The attached Fourth Division was assigned no routine position. Sherman addressed a number of issues to his division commanders on 13 December, two of which were to become contentious. First and foremost, they must be ready to depart on the 18th, no excuses would be accepted. Additionally, Sherman directed that the divisions must bring the necessary equipment to build bridges.[45] The haste with which the force was expected to prepare and the impact of this haste on the availability of bridging would be critical during the battle at Chickasaw Bayou and would be a source of criticism against Sherman.

On the 18th Sherman issued final orders detailing the procedures for boats on the river and specified some rules of engagement for the force. The illegal trade in cotton with the

Confederates was a problem in all operations. Sherman specifically forbade all such trade. The only cotton that could be confiscated and not burned was that necessary for use as bulwarks on the boats. Sherman had a festering hatred for newspaper reporters stemming from accusations they had previously made concerning his sanity. On this expedition he ordered that no newsmen would come aboard and if they did they would be conscripted. If they wrote a report they would be treated as a spy. In defiance of these orders, Thomas W. Knox, correspondent of the *New York Herald* stole aboard. Enroute he was discovered and only escaped Sherman's justice by obtaining refuge on Porter's flagship. As the only reporter on the expedition and treated in this manner, he would not shed a good light on Sherman's activities and would be a continuous source of criticism.[46]

Low waters on the Mississippi River delayed the arrival of many of the steamboats and gunboats from Cairo forcing a delay on the 18th and causing Sherman to set a new departure date for the 20th. As waters began to rise on the 18th, Porter was able to arrive from Cairo and begin active planning with Sherman. By the 19th, Sherman had the boats he needed to load his force and depart on the 20th. Sherman sent the first group of boats to Helena bringing Steele's total to nineteen. As the remaining boats arrived in Memphis he allocated sixteen to the

First Division with one additional, the steamboat Forest Queen, for his command group. The Second Division received eleven, and the Third Division thirteen. Porter organized his gunboats into two divisions each consisting of six gunboats.[47]

For the Union soldiers at Memphis the activities did not appear coherent or particularly well planned. When the fleet began to move out on the 20th, not all the required boats had arrived as Sherman had thought. Brigadier General A.J. Smith's First Division had to load hurriedly on late arriving boats and did not depart until the 21st.[48] In the confusion and excitement of the departure regimental officers throughout Sherman's army allowed vital equipment to be left behind. On the steamboat Westmoreland drunken soldiers of the 55th Illinois Volunteer Regiment, Fourth Brigade, Second Division hindered loading operations as officers struggled to get them aboard. A carnival atmosphere permeated this army of regiments largely untested in battle.[49] Many regiments departed short of officers and men. Some regiments had only junior officers or noncommissioned officers in the key positions. On the books these units were at full strength. In fact, many officers were absent, other soldiers on detached duty or sick. The 83d Indiana Volunteer Infantry Regiment in the Third Brigade, Second Division had to leave a good number of its measle stricken men in Memphis as they boarded the steamer Sioux City.[50]

A minor guerrilla raid on Memphis on the 19th added to the chaotic scene. A small mounted irregular force made a run into the town, set fires, stole horses and was pursued by the 8th Mississippi Cavalry Regiment. Although ineffective, the raid must have provided some intelligence to the Confederates as to the massive boat and troop build up.[51]

Sherman dispatched his final message to Grant from Memphis on 19 December. Sherman planned to leave Memphis in advance of his army on the 20th to move to Helena to ensure that Steele's force was ready, that Friars Point was garrisoned, and that a cavalry force was operating on the Tallahatchie. Sherman expected to depart Helena with Steele on the 21st. He planned to be at the Yazoo by the 25th. Sherman concluded his message by emphasizing that he was prepared to resupply Grant from the Yazoo River, also as previously specified.[52]

CONFEDERATE CAVALRY RAIDS ON GRANT

As Sherman's amphibious wing loaded ships on 20 December, twin cavalry raids were striking Grant's rear. Forrest's attack and destruction of the railroad at Jackson, Tennessee, on 18 and 19 December severed Grant completely from communications with everyone outside his force in northern Mississippi. Grant immediately halted his army ordering Major General James B. McPherson to advance no farther until further directions. Ominously, reports reached Grant from McPherson that a heavy column of cavalry was seen departing from Grenada. Grant immediately alerted his commanders at Holly Springs, Davis' Mill, Grand Junction, La Grange, and Bolivar to be prepared for a heavy cavalry force moving north to cut the lines of communications.[53]

Forrest's attack stopped Grant's advance as he cut Grant's only supply line. The next Confederate stroke put Grant into retreat. Van Dorn's cavalry force, eluding the pursuing Union cavalry, swept into Holly Springs on 20 December destroying enormous stores of supplies. Holly Springs was Grant's forward supply depot on the end of his long supply tether to Columbus, Kentucky. Van Dorn was fortunate that Grant's commander at Holly Springs could not have been worse. Post Commander, Colonel R.C. Murphy, already on probation for misconduct in battle, was caught napping, an act of "inconceivable imbecility" considering the warning he had already received.[54]

As Van Dorn slipped north continuing to destroy track on the Tennessee and Ohio Railroad, Grant initiated a retreat, ordering McPherson to fall back with his command to the north side of the Tallahatchie River. Simultaneously, Grant would try to push his cavalry towards Grenada to "keep up the idea of an advance as much as possible."[55]

By the 21st, Grant was hearing rumors of an advance by Braxton Bragg towards Corinth. Grant ordered two of his divisions to move there to strengthen the defenses. Grant speculated that the whole force might be needed there so he planned to hold temporarily on the line of the Tallahatchie River. If Bragg's attack did not occur, Grant planned to move two divisions to Memphis and two to Bolivar, the intent being to reinforce the amphibious wing while conducting a holding action in the vicinity of the Tallahatchie.

By the 23d, Grant had ascertained some of the damage done to his supply line and confirmed that Bragg's attack was a hoax. Grant held firm on the Tallahatchie, while his cavalry pursued Van Dorn in Mississippi and Forrest in west Tennessee.[56] Grant would not move until his supply line was repaired or he developed a new line of supply. Why didn't Grant simply abandon his line of communications at this point and continue to pressure Pemberton? At first it was clearly the threat he felt from Bragg at Corinth. When this threat dissipated he had to assess his current supply status. The loss of Holly Springs and the railroads to his rear meant he had no supply line. Grant said in his memoirs that:

> It should be remembered that at the time I speak of it had not been demonstrated that an army could operate in an enemy's territory depending on the country for supplies.[57]

Additionally, the Union plan called for no advance south of the Yalabusha, unless Pemberton were falling back. By the 23d Grant had not done anything that would cripple the campaign. He still held on the Tallahatchie, seeking to open a new supply line to Memphis. Grant would fail in his responsibilities when he did not pressure Pemberton in any way during Sherman's attack, enabling Pemberton to thin out his forces. Grant may not have had supplies from his rear, but the plan had been developed for his resupply on the Yazoo by Sherman for just such an eventuality. The key to success of the whole plan was not to allow reinforcements to get to the Yazoo.

A fortuitous byproduct of the raids was that the loss of communications caused Grant's 18 December message to McClernand and Sherman to be delayed. Sherman would leave Memphis on the 20th not having received the new orders, fighting the battle as the Commander, Right Wing, Thirteenth Army Corps although that designation had been eliminated on the 18th. McClernand would languish at Springfield still awaiting orders. McClernand's orders would finally come on 23 December and then only after he again telegraphed Stanton. Halleck had not sent orders to McClernand and Stanton personally had to order McClernand forward.

JOINT OPERATIONS ON THE RIVER

Since the loss of the Cairo on the Yazoo on 12 December, Navy operations had been light. Although Porter had positioned forces at the mouth of the Yazoo, Confederate concern about their activities was decreasing with their relative inactivity. Following Porter's arrival at Memphis, Naval activities dramatically increased. On 20 December, Porter ordered Lieutenant Commander William Gwin, commanding the U.S.S. Benton, to proceed from Helena, Arkansas, to the Yazoo. Once there he was to take command of elements of Captain Walke's fleet and sortie up the Yazoo. His mission was to clear torpedoes and obstructions in order to clear the channel for the army troop transports to land. Though not specifically told how far to go, the intent was to clear as high up the river as possible, at a minimum providing clear landing sites. Porter ordered Gwin to provide topographical observations and assigned him a Coast Survey officer to assist in the effort. Finally, Porter stressed to Gwin "to impress the enemy with the idea that the boats are endeavoring to pass up the river, not to secure a landing for troops."[58]

Sherman arrived in Helena ahead of the convoy on the 20th. Although delayed for two days by the low waters, from his perspective everything was going relatively smoothly for the amphibious wing at Memphis. The same could not be said for the element from Helena. Steele was in complete readiness to embark on the 20th; however, Gorman had completely failed to prepare his part of the operation. Sherman had to energize him to send the infantry force across the Mississippi to secure the rendezvous site at Friars Point and to dispatch the 2,000 man cavalry force meant to be operating on Pemberton's flank along the Tallahatchie. Gorman only managed to get these forces in place by the 24th, too late to be of any value.[59]

By mid day on the 21st, the amphibious wing was on the Mississippi River in its entirety. The gunboats had gone down river to prepare the Yazoo on the 20th. By 9 A.M. on the 21st, Morgan L. Smith's Second Division and George W. Morgan's Third Division had passed Helena to the first rendezvous at Friars Point. During the passing, M.L. Smith reported to Sherman that twenty five Union soldiers had come into Memphis on the 20th having barely escaped capture by the Confederates at Holly Springs.[60] Critics have pointed to this episode, blaming Sherman for continuing the operation when he should have used better judgement and delayed to find out the true situation with Grant. Sherman did not know what credence to place in the reports and chose to accept that without any other guidance he would continue the mission. Sherman had no knowledge of Forrest's raid deep in Grant's rear and therefore did not see any real danger from an attack on Holly

Springs. Furthermore, he had anticipated resupplying Grant's force on the Yazoo with the expectation that Grant would have to break from his supply lines if pursuit of Pemberton became necessary. Sherman was not alone in his expectation that Grant would resupply at the Yazoo River regardless of the cavalry raids.

With Grant completely cut off from Washington, Halleck attempted to get status reports from commanders on the periphery of Forrest's raid. Captain Henry S. Fitch, Assistant Quartermaster at Cairo, Illinois, served as a message relay for Sherman just prior to his departure from Memphis. Seeking to reassure Halleck as to Grant's probable actions as a result of the breaking of his lines of communications, Fitch wrote:

> It may not be unimportant to know that General Sherman took with him 1,600,000 rations, or 600,000 more than originally intended, anticipating, as I understood, the possibility of General Grant being compelled to draw supplies from him for a short time in case of accident to his railroad communication.[61]

Sherman, unlike Grant, had no conceptual problem with the movement of armies independent of established supply lines.

By 22 December, Sherman's entire force was rendezvoused at Friars Point where final preparations for the joint movement were accomplished and Sherman was able to issue the campaign plan and tentative tactical plan to his division commanders. The purpose of the operation he identified was to "secure the navigation of the Mississippi River and its main branches, and to hold them as military channels of communication and for commercial purposes."[62] The key to success of this operation was the seizure of Vicksburg in a concerted action in which the amphibious wing was just one element. Assisting and acting "in perfect harmony with the other" was a force under Banks moving north from New Orleans; Grant with the main body of the Thirteenth Army Corps moving southward; and the naval squadron of gunboats under Porter. Sherman told his commanders that Grant was moving on the Yalabusha and although "the railroad to his rear, by which he drew his supplies, was reported to be seriously damaged" he did not expect him to be thwarted but would make the river line of communications even more essential.[64] Sherman believed that Grant would find a retreating Pemberton and would pursue him down the high ridge between the Big Black River and the Yazoo River, an avenue that offered the best axis of attack from Grenada to the Yazoo. Sherman's intent was to reduce Vicksburg from the river, secure the land between the Yazoo and the Big Black River, and then attack Pemberton's army at Jackson, Mississippi, or Vicksburg as the opportunities arose.[65]

Sherman was not prepared to give detailed tactical directives. He told his commanders that the force would again rendezvous at Gaines Landing, Arkansas, from which he would dispatch his divisions separately to Milliken's Bend just short of the Yazoo. At Milliken's Bend Sherman intended to dispatch a brigade to destroy the Vicksburg and Shreveport Railroad (western wing of the Southern Railroad) and then to move to the mouth of the Yazoo. At the Yazoo Sherman expected to receive the latest intelligence from the navy, to land the force on the Mississippi side, and to attack to reach the point where the Vicksburg and Jackson Railroad (eastern wing of the Southern Railroad) crossed the Big Black. Once there, Sherman planned to attack Vicksburg in conjunction with a naval bombardment. Sherman anticipated that it would be necessary to resupply Grant up the Yazoo River, and he planned for the reduction of the batteries at Haynes' Bluff in order to ascend with his supply boats.[66] Sherman provided no further tactical instructions promising only to do so in "due season."[67] Sherman provided each of his commanders a detailed map and instructed them to study it and prepare all equipment so that there would be no shortage once ashore. Although specifically not reminding his commanders to take the pontoons ashore, a simple study of the map he provided shows the swampy nature of the terrain laced with numerous streams and bayous. This alone should have dictated the necessity for taking bridging as common sense. It would prove not to be the case.

Sherman's command ship the Forest Queen led the armada out of Friars Point followed closely by the divisions in numerical order. Under orders to respond to attack and not overly concerned with achieving surprise, the Union soldiers wrecked havoc as they moved southward. Soldiers of the Eighty Third Ohio Volunteer Infantry heard a rumor that a Union man had been put in a barrel and rolled in the river by the towns people of Friars Point. In retaliation they reduced the town to ashes. At Napoleon the boats received light gunfire which resulted in immediate retaliation by the gunboats.[68] Throughout the expedition any gunfire from the banks resulted in crop destruction and the burning of homes and farm buildings. Sherman's armada cut a swathe of destruction on both banks of the river.

Porter's gunboat operations were stepped up on 23 December. Lieutenant Commander John G. Walker, commander of the U.S.S. Baron De Kalb, led an expedition up the Yazoo and began intensive river clearing operations. These operations to clear the channel were augmented by the arrival that same day of the eight gunboats under the command of Lieutenant Commander Gwin and continued throughout the campaign. By the 26th, the gunboats had been able to clear only to the wreck of the <u>Cairo,</u> unable to clear to the vicinity of Snyder's Bluff due to heavy fire.[69]

The transport fleet cleared Gaines Landing and began arriving at Milliken's Bend on the evening of 24 December. Sherman immediately issued orders to Brigadier General Andrew J. Smith to detach a brigade from his lead First Division to cut the Vicksburg and Shreveport Railroad. The loss of this railroad would cost the Confederacy the main artery of supply to the cattle and wheat of Texas and cut the link between Holmes's army and Pemberton's.[70] A.J. Smith ordered his First Brigade under Brigadier General Stephen G. Burbridge to draw two days rations and prepare to depart on the morning of the 25th. Early that morning, Burbridge set out with six infantry regiments, two cavalry companies, and one artillery piece west towards the railroad at Dallas Station, Louisiana.[71] Burbridge's hard marching infantry moved twenty six miles reaching Dallas Station in early afternoon where they "immediately began the work of destruction."[72] Burbridge dispatched an element of the Sixth Missouri Cavalry to Delhi, twelve miles away, and smaller cavalry detachments were sent to other outlying towns. Everywhere the cavalry was sent they destroyed cotton, buildings, and as much of the railroad line as was possible. Under continual harassment from Confederate cavalry, Burbridge began his movement back to Milliken's Bend by mid morning on the 26th. By midnight his force began loading on the boats, having marched and fought seventy five miles in thirty six hours.[73] Burbridge's expedition was tremendously successful, destroying three railroad bridges, a mile of road, 1,000 bales of cotton, huge granaries, and capturing many horses and mules.[74] He showed very clearly just what Sherman had said could be done if the Mississippi were controlled by the Union and in the final battle report Sherman would point to this operation as an important success in an otherwise unsuccessful campaign. With the exception of Burbridge's artillery "gun toters," and some cavalry elements, A.J. Smith's division began its movement from Milliken's Bend to the Yazoo on the morning of the 27th.[75]

As Burbridge's brigade was set in motion, Sherman initiated his movement on the Yazoo. Sherman instructed A.J. Smith to remain at Milliken's Bend to await the return of his First Brigade. On the 25th as promised to Grant, Sherman moved the whole force opposite the mouth the Yazoo, landing at Young's Point on the west bank of the Mississippi River. At this point he ordered Brigadier General Morgan L. Smith to dispatch a brigade to destroy the Vicksburg and Shreveport Railroad at a point nearer Vicksburg.[76] Four Regiments of the Second Division disembarked at 2:00 P.M.

and completed the thirteen mile foray into Louisiana at about 10:00 P.M., destroying a considerable amount of railroad track.[77]

With his army and naval forces congregated at the mouth of the Yazoo, Sherman coordinated his initial tactical actions. Having no other source of information, Sherman relied on the information Porter's naval officers could provide on the topography and the enemy situation. From this meeting it was clear that the river was not cleared up to the best point of landing at Snyder's Bluff due to the heavy defenses on the high ground and the large number of torpedo's in the channel.[78] Consequently, Sherman directed that the landing would take place approximately twelve miles up the Yazoo River on the east bank in the vicinity of Johnson's plantation. The fleet would depart at 8:00 A.M. on 26 December under gunboat escort and with two companies on each boat armed to return fire on the bank.

The Third Division under G.W. Morgan would lead, landing at the upper end of Johnson's plantation immediately sending one brigade towards Mrs. Lakes's plantation. The Fourth Division under Steele would follow, land at Johnson's plantation and send one brigade on the Vicksburg Road about two miles inland. M.L. Smith would follow the Fourth Division, landing just below. Since M.L. Smith was still involved in destroying the railroad opposite the Yazoo, his remaining brigade under Brigadier General David Stuart would act alone. A.J. Smith's First Division would be the trail element and would disembark above Bunch's Saw Mill.

Although not on any maps, this point was west of M.L. Smith's landing site.[79] With these simple instructions the Battle of Chickasaw Bayou commenced.

CONFEDERATE COUNTERMOVES

Sherman's preparations at Memphis could not be concealed from the thousands of loyal Confederates in the area. Whether from this source or as a result of the cavalry raid on Memphis, Pemberton was apprised on 21 December of a large fleet of gunboats and transports moving down the Mississippi River "for the supposed purpose of attacking Vicksburg.[80] Pemberton immediately dispatched Vaughn's Tennessee Brigade to Vicksburg and alerted Price, then in front of Grant at Grenada, to be prepared to reinforce also.[81]

By Christmas Eve, there was no doubt in Pemberton's mind as to what the Union forces were trying to do. For almost a week Union gunboats had been reconnoitering and removing torpedoes on the Yazoo. To Brigadier General Stephen D. Lee, commander of the Provisional Division at Vicksburg, this activity "indicated the probable point of attack", simplifying their planning and preparations.[82] Colonel Wirt Adams, commanding a Confederate cavalry force, reported to Pemberton on the 24th that forty-five enemy transports and ten gunboats passed Friars Point on the 22d.[83] No doubt the Union attempt to teach that town a lesson contributed to the "signature" of the expedition. With this information Pemberton dispatched Brigadier General John Gregg's brigade of Price's Corps to Vicksburg.[84]

Anticipdting an amphibious operation from the north, the Confederates had established a telegraph station on the Mississippi River on the bank opposite Vicksburg. This station, commanded by Colonel Phillip H. Fall, was connected to a small observation station sixty five miles north of Vicksburg in the vicinity of Lake Providence. The operator at that station, Major L.L. Daniel, was to report only the Union river traffic. The importance of this system to the Confederates is certainly reflected in the ranks of the two individuals placed in command of these facilities. At 8:45 P.M., 24 December, Major Daniel observed the entire river force pass his site. Barely beating a small Union cavalry troop sent to destroy the wires, he managed to get his message through to Colonel Fall. Receiving the information at his Christmas Eve Ball, Major General M.L. Smith immediately launched into his final preparations for the Union assault.[85]

In the early morning hours of 25 December, Major General M.L. Smith ordered Brigadier General S.D. Lee to command the line of battle along the Walnut Hills north of Vicksburg to Snyder's Bluff orienting along the country road at the foot of the hills. Union gunboat activity had simplified the planning for Smith. He knew that the attack would come on the Yazoo. Controlling only 6,500 men in Vicksburg, Smith dispatched Lee with six regiments of infantry and two artillery batteries to defend along Walnut Hills. This left him only 1,000 artillery troops and the 27th Louisiana Infantry of 600 men to defend fortress Vicksburg. Smith could count on two brigades arriving from Pemberton's army and a division enroute from General Bragg.[86] Every moment wasted by the Union at this point turned the advantage to the Confederacy. As Smith ordered Lee to the trenches, Pemberton shifted his headquarters to Vicksburg.[87] With no pressure from Grant in north central Mississippi, Pemberton felt confident enough to order Major General Dabney H. Maury with all but one brigade of his First Division to move from Grenada to Vicksburg.[87]

Grant's failure to pin Pemberton's army on the Yalabusha was becoming crucial to the attainment of Confederate defensive parity against Sherman.

The opening phases of the Chickasaw Bayou campaign did not bode well for the Union forces and would continue to trouble the operation until its climax. The Confederate cavalry raids were the key elements of the defensive strategy and were executed flawlessly. The fact that they were so successful did not excuse Grant from retreating and thereby completely failing in his obligation to support Sherman's river operation. Grant's demonstrations on the Yalabusha and if necessary an offensive from that line was the absolute key to success for the operation. Although it was hoped that an expedition from New Orleans would support, only Grant would be able to prevent serious reinforcement of Vicksburg. By 25 December his failure allowed Pemberton to shift two brigades and most of one division from central Mississippi to Vicksburg.

Sherman has been blamed for failing to delay the operation following news of Van Dorn's strike at Holly Springs in order to await furthur guidance from Grant. He has been blamed for trying too hard to supersede McClernand, and therefore made a rash decision to continue the operation. In fact, Sherman and Grant had planned for the resupply and, to Sherman, Grant was in no danger. Sherman knew nothing of Forrest's attack, an event that very likely would have caused Sherman to establish contact with Grant before continuing. Under the circumstances, Sherman had prudently judged the situation; he failed to judge properly Grant.

The Union gunboat activity had a tremendous impact on

the operation. Althougn absolutely necessary, the complete lack of any deceptive measures enabled the Confederates to identify the exact points of debarkation. As will be seen, they were able to employ this information to their great advantage in the tactical preparation of the battlefield. Porter knew that the invasion would be executed on the Yazoo as early as November. With more deliberation, he certainly could have masked his efforts or at least developed a pattern of activity that would not have resulted in the tremendous surge just as the entire amphibious wing moved down river.

The Confederates acted with a sense of purpose that was not evident in the Union camp. While Union forces leisurely moved down river, amply advertising their activities, Confederate forces frantically repositioned forces throughout the theater of operations. The initiation of the reinforcements from Bragg's army were critical to Pemberton's hard battling army in central Mississippi. The ability to augment these forces with elements of Price's corps was to turn the tide. Although Confederate forces were restricted to one east-west railroad out of Vicksburg and one north-south railroad to Grenada, Confederate commanders kept these systems busy with the shifting of troops.

Finally, a tremendous advantage in the Confederate operations was the constant stream of intelligence. Union forces operated in hostile territory and could hope to receive no accurate information from the locals.

Confederate forces certainly gleaned excellent information not only from their network of guerrillas, cavalry, and river watchers, but also from a very loyal population inflamed by Union excesses.

As Union soldiers made final preparations to come ashore, they were completely unaware that a race was on. Confederate forces, although poorly prepared to defend against them, used every minute to improve their defenses. Although the odds for success were starting to shift to the Confederacy, bold action by Sherman could still win the battle.

ENDNOTES

1. Carl Sandburg, Abraham Lincoln-The War Years (New York: Harcourt, Brace & Co., 1939), 106.

2. The War of Rebellion: A Compilation of the Official Records of the Union and Confederate Armies 128 vols. (Washington: Government Printing Office, 1880-1901) Series I, Vol. XVII, Part 1: 472. (Cited hereafter as OR.)

3. Ibid., 473

4. Ibid.

5. lbid., 4 & 601.

6. William T. Sherman, Memoirs of General W.T. Sherman

(New York: The Library of America, 1990), 304-305.

7. OR, Series I, Vol. XVII,   Part 1, 474.

8. U.S. Grant, The Personal Memoirs of U.S. Grant (New York: The World Publishing Co., 1952), 225.

9. OR, Series I, Vol.   XVII, Part 1, 474.

10. OR, Series I, Vol. XVII,   Part 2, 392-393.

11. OR, Series I, Vol. XVII,   Part 1, 474.

12. Sherman,   307-308.

13. OR, Series I, Vol. XVII,   Part 2, 392.

14. OR, Series I, Vol. XVII,   Part 1, 601.

15. Ibid., 602.

16. OR, Series I, Vol. XVII,   Part 1, 617 and Part 2, 402-403.

17. OR, Series I, Vol. XVII, Part 1, 602.

18. OR, Series I, Vol. XVII, Part 2, 406-407.

19. Ibid.

20. Ibid., 410.

21. Ibid., 414.

22. Ibid.

23. The War of Rebellion: A Compilation of the Official Records of the Union and Confederate Navies, 31 vols. (Washington: Government Printing Office, 1894-1922) series I, Vol. XXIII: 395-396. (Cited hereafter as ORN).

24. Ibid., 540,544.

25. Ibid., 540, 546.

26. Ibid., 541.

27. <u>OR</u>, Series I, Vol. XVII, Part 2, 401, 413.

28. Ibid., 415, 420.

29. <u>OR</u>, Series I, Vol. XVII, Part 1, 476 & Part 2, 432.

30. <u>OR</u>, Series I, Vol. XVII, Part 1, 420.

31. <u>OR</u>, Series I, Vol. XVII, Part 2, 425.

32. Ibid., 436.

33. Ibid., 780.

34. Joseph E. Johnston, <u>Narrative of Military Operations During the Civil War</u> (Bloomington: Indiana University Press, 1959), 151 and <u>OR</u>, Series I, Vol. XVII, Part 2, 781.

35. Archer Jones, <u>Confederate Strategy from Shiloh to Vicksburg</u> (Baton Rouge: Louisiana University Press, 1961), 117.

36. Johnston, 151-152.

37. Jones, 125.

38. <u>OR</u>, Series I, Vol. XVII, Part 2, 786-787.

39. Ibid., 793.

40. Ibid., 778.

41. Robert G. Hartje, <u>Van Dorn</u> (Charlotte, N.C.: Vanderbilt University Press, 1967), 255.

42. <u>OR</u>, Series I, Vol. XVII, Part 2, 798.

43. <u>OR</u>, Series I, Vol. XVII, Part 1, 593.

44. Johnston, 153.

45. OR, Series I, Vol. XVII, Part 1, 617.

46. OR, Series I, Vol. XVII, Part 1, 619-620 and Sylvanus Cadwallader, Three Years with Grant (New York: Alfred A. Knopf, 1956), 45.

47. ORN, Series I, Vol. XXIII, 558, 563-564.

48. OR, Series I, Vol. XVII, Part 1, 627.

49. Committee of the Regiment, The Story of the Fifty Fifth Regiment Illinois Volunteer Infantry, (Clinton, Mass: W.J. Coulter, 1887), 186.

50. Joseph J. Grecian, History of the 83d Regiment Indiana Volunteer Infantry, (Cincinnati, 1865), 17.

51. Henry C. Bear, The Civil War Letters of Henry C. Bear ed. Wayne C. Temple, (Harrogate, Tenn.: Lincoln Memorial University Press, 1961), 13.

52. OR, Series I, Vol. XVII, Part 1, 603-604.

53. OR, Series I, Vol. XVII, Part 2, 435, 438-439.

54. Bruce Catton, Grant Moves South (Boston: Little, Brown and Co., 1960), 340 and Owen J. Hopkins, Under the Flag of the Nation Diaries and Letters of a Yankee Volunteer in the Civil War ed. Otto F. Bond, (Columbus: Ohio State University Press, 1961), 45.

55. OR, Series I, Vol. XVII, Part 2, 445.

56. Ibid., 464.

57. Grant, 225.

58. <u>ORN</u>, Series I, Vol. XXIII, 567,569.

59. <u>OR</u>, Series I, Vol XVII, Part 1, 604-605, and Part 2, 464.

60. <u>OR</u>, Series I, Vol XVII, Part 1, 604.

61. <u>OR</u>, Series I, Vol. XVII, Part 2, 480.

62. <u>OR</u>, Series I, Vol XVII, Part 1, 616.

63. Sherman, 310.

64. Ibid.

65. Ibid., 311.

66. Ibid.

67. <u>OR</u>, Series I, Vol XVII, Part 1, 617.

68. Thomas B. Marshall, History of the Eighty Third Ohio Volunteer Infantry (Cincinnati: The Eighty Third Ohio Volunteer Infantry Association, 1913), 49.

69. <u>ORN</u>, Series I, Vol. XXIII, 569-570, 573.

70. Marshall, 50.

71. <u>OR</u>, Series I, Vol. XVII, Part 1, 627.

72. Marshall, 50.

73. <u>OR</u>, Series I, Vol. XVII, Part 1, 630.

74. Ibid., 627.

75. Marshall, 50.

76. <u>OR</u>, Series I, Vol. XVII, Part 1, 605.

77. Bear, 19.

78. <u>OR</u>, Series I, Vol. XVII, Part 1, 605.

79. Ibid., 620.

80. Ibid., 666.

81. OR, Series I, Vol. XVII, Part 1, 661 and Part 2, 800.

82. OR, Series I, Vol. XVII, Part 2, 803.

83. Stephen D. Lee, "The Campaign of General Grant and Sherman against Vicksburg in December 1862 and January 1st and 2d, 1863, known as the 'Chickasaw Bayou Campaign' " in Publications of the Mississippi Historical Society, ed. Franklin L. Riley, (Oxford, Mississippi: Harrisburg Publishing Co., 1902) IV: 23.

84. OR, Series I, Vol. XVII, Part 1, 666.

85. Stephen D. Lee, "Details of Important Work by Two Confederate Telegraph Operators, Christmas Eve, 1862, Which Prevented the Almost Complete Surprise of the Confederate Army at Vicksburg" in Publications of the Mississippi Historical Society, ed. Franklin L. Riley, (Oxford, Mississippi: Harrisburg Publishing Co., 1902) VIII: 53-54.

86. Lee, "The Campaign," 24.

87. Dabney H. Maury, Recollections of a Virginian in the Mexican, Indian and Civil Wars (New York: Charles Scribner's Sons, 1894), 168 and OR, Series I, Vol. XVII, Part 2, 804.

CHAPTER THREE - THE BATTLE AT CHICKASAW BAYOU

TACTICAL COMBAT OPERATIONS - THE OPENING MOVES - 26 DECEMBER-28 DECEMBER 1862

"Boys! Boys! This is not war, this is murder."
Brigadier General Stephen D. Lee Chickasaw
Bayou, December 1862.[1]

Sherman's amphibious wing was preparing to attack a tiny Confederate force defending in formidably difficult terrain. The alien terrain was to affect Sherman's plans for the entire battle and ultimately the natural terrain features, augmented by lightly manned Confederate defensive works, stymied the main attack. On 26 December 1862 the key to success at the tactical level was for the Union forces to act boldly and quickly.

THE BATTLEFIELD

The line of battle assigned to Brigadier General S.D. Lee from Vicksburg to Snyder's Bluff was naturally ideal for defensive positions. Running northeast from the city was a series of high bluffs known as Walnut Hills which formed the first plateau between the Mississippi River and the interior of the state of Mississippi. This plateau extended well into north central Mississippi and provided the natural avenue of movement along the river. At the base of these hills, at the northern juncture of the Mississippi River and Vicksburg, was a race course about two miles north of the city. From this race course north to Snyder's Mill, closely following the base of the bluffs, was an elevated dirt road known as the Valley Road. The area between the Yazoo River and the Valley Road was a maze of swamps, bayous, and old river beds. From the Yazoo juncture with the Mississippi River, the first open and dry ground suitable for a landing to approach the city from the north was twelve miles upriver at the abandoned Johnson's plantation. The intervening terrain was heavily wooded and subject to river overflow, impossible for large army movements. This heavily wooded section of country was naturally separated from Johnson's plantation by an old channel of the Mississippi or the Yazoo and was known as the Old River.

Approximately five miles to the east of the Old River was another channel from the Yazoo running generally south to the Walnut Hills. This bayou, known as the Chickasaw Bayou, turned northeast at the base of the bluffs, disappearing into the hills. At the point where the Chickasaw Bayou first strikes the base of the hills, another broad and shallow bayou called Fishing Lake on Confederate maps, or McNutt Lake on Union maps, followed the base of the hills south west past the race course back into the jungled Old River region. The effect of these three bayous was to create a triangular island. The Yazoo River formed the northern base of this island. The Old River in the west, and the Chickasaw Bayou in the east formed a funnel to the apex of the triangle at the McNutt Lake at the base of Walnut Hills.

Between the Chickasaw Bayou and Snyder's Bluff was a heavily vegetated and swampy region generally unsuitable for landing except in the immediate vicinity of Snyder's Bluff. In this entire area the only route from the Yazoo to the Walnut Hills other than Snyder's Bluff was along a levee known as Blake's Levee. This levee originated at the Yazoo just north of the mouth of the Chickasaw Bayou, oriented south east towards the bluff and was built along the eastern side of Thompson Lake. Thompson Lake followed the same general course to the bluffs, paralleling Chickasaw Bayou, eventually petering out near the point where the Chickasaw Bayou cut into the bluffs. The levee did not cross the Chickasaw Bayou at the base of the hills, instead a rough corduroy road extended from the levee, across the bayou, to the Valley Road.[2]

Between the race course and Snyder's Bluff there were only five ways to approach Walnut Hills from the Yazoo River without building bridges or crossing swamps. The Snyder's

94

Bluff area, thirteen miles from Vicksburg, offered the best landing site with the closest approach to the bluff from the Yazoo River. Blake's Levee offered the only other means to approach the bluffs north of Chickasaw Bayou. Following along Chickasaw Bayou from Johnson's plantation was a narrow road leading to and crossing the point where McNutt Lake joined the Chickasaw Bayou at the base of the hills. This area was part of what was known as Mrs. Lake's plantation, with the plantation house situated at roughly the midpoint along Chickasaw Bayou. Immediately to the west of this crossing point McNutt Lake formed its major channel having a width of eighty feet. Pontoon bridging was the only way to cross this obstacle. Several miles to the southwest was a 200 yard dry ford of McNutt Lake opposite an old Indian Mound at the base of the bluffs. The approach to this ford was along a small road that could be reached along roads from Mrs. Lake's plantation and Johnson's plantation. The fifth means to approach the hills was a road known as the Vicksburg Road leading from Johnson's plantation to the race course which cut across the bayou into Vicksburg. With the exception of the Snyder's Bluff approach, each of these avenues required crossing McNutt Lake, Chickasaw Bayou or a dry portion of either bayou immediately adjacent to the bluffs. These water courses, whether wet or dry, had generally sloping banks on the northern side, with very steep embankments on the side nearest the bluffs. The Valley Road at the top of this steep embankment was designed to serve as a levee and thus added significantly to the obstacle and vertical ascent.[3]

S.D. LEE TAKES OVER

Despite all the warning and knowledge of Union plans, Lee found the defensive preparations woefully inadequate along the line he was ordered to defend. "Not a spade of dirt had been thrown up along this entire line and there were no entrenchments nor covered batteries" lamented Lee years later.[4] The only apparent preparations were at Snyder's Bluff and extensive timber abatis blocking the Vicksburg Road at the race course. Lee immediately set to work to correct the problem. With a large force of slaves he began defensive preparations at the most likely avenues over which Union forces had to move. The terrain could not have been better suited for hasty work; it was obvious to Lee the Union forces must attack at only four points other than the well defended batteries at Snyder's Bluff. Because these points could be controlled by Confederate fire from the Valley Road, Lee chose to defend at the base of the hills rather than defend along the military crest. This forward defense was ideal under the circumstances in that each crossing point over McNutt Lake or Chickasaw Bayou could be contested from high ground created by the Valley Road and the Indian Mound. Lee's labor force dug rifle and gun pits at the race course, at the Indian Mound, at the intersection of McNutt Lake and Chickasaw Bayou, and opposite Blake's Levee. At the two dry crossing sites west of Chickasaw Bayou, Lee created an impenetrable tangle of felled timber. Lee continued the frantic defensive work with his slave force until the evening of 27 December, the first day Union forces threatened the bluffs.[5]

By the early morning of 26 December Lee had detailed his small force, known as the Provisional Division, to cover the key approaches relying heavily on the use of abatis to cover areas he could not immediately physically occupy. At the Indian Mound he placed the 31st Louisiana with two guns from the Mississippi Regiment of Light Artillery. At Chickasaw Bayou Lee positioned four regiments and a battery of eight guns. Between the Indian Mound and the Bayou, Lee held his final regiment in rifle pits. At Snyder's Bluff, were two regiments of infantry and artillery relatively immobilized by the necessity to defend the fortifications. Lee's force was a meager 2700 men to combat Sherman's 30,000.[6] Until reinforcements arrived, Lee had no troops occupying positions at the race course or near Blake's Levee.

UNION LANDING - 26 DECEMBER

In accordance with the previous days plan, the troop transports of Brigadier General G.W. Morgan's Third Division moved into the Yazoo at 8:00 A.M.. The three brigades of the division unloaded just north of Johnson's plantation near the Boat Slough west of Chickasaw Bayou. As directed by Sherman in his orders of 25 December, Morgan immediately ordered Colonel John F. DeCourcy, commanding the Third Brigade, to push forward and recon along the Chickasaw Bayou for a distance of a mile and a half.[7]

This first landing did not go unnoticed by Confederate scouts who flashed the information to S.D. Lee. Lee began the first in a series of ad hoc brigadings of the regiments of his Provisional Division. Lee responded to crisis at threatened points by creating brigades as regiments became available. Lee directed Colonel William T. Withers of the First Mississippi Light Artillery to take charge of the defenses at Chickasaw Bayou and to gather a force and establish a forward defensive outpost at Mrs. Lake's plantation house to delay the Union advance.[8] Withers's force consisted of the 17th Louisiana Regiment, the 26th Louisiana Regiment, two companies of the 46th Mississippi Regiment, and a section of Captain J. L. Wofford's Company D, First Mississippi Light Artillery. Withers immediately sent the 26th Louisiana and the two companies of the 46th Mississippi north of the plantation house to the Lake plantation cotton gin to act as skirmishers while the remainder of his force stayed in position near Mrs. Lake's house.[9]

With no cavalry or supporting artillery, DeCourcy's brigade moved in column towards Mrs. Lake's plantation striking the skirmishers of the 26th Louisiana and 46th Mississippi near the cotton gin. Quickly forming into line of battle, DeCourcy pressed the Confederates to the plantation house. The timely arrival of a twelve pounder from Wofford's section forced DeCourcy to stop his advance and seek shelter. Without artillery of his own, he could not advance. By nightfall, DeCourcy had pulled back to a position north of the cotton gin. In the late evening Withers took advantage of the respite to relieve the 26th Louisiana with the 17th. Withers positioned the 26th on the west side of the Chickasaw Bayou behind the protection of a levee to the rear of Mrs. Lake's house.[10]

Colonel Daniel W. Lindsay, commanding the Second Brigade of the Third Division, landed behind DeCourcy's brigade. Morgan directed him to place his brigade in a bivouac on the bank of the Yazoo.[11] Colonel Lionel A. Sheldon, commanding the First Brigade of the Third Division, bivouacked on the bank of the Yazoo to the west of Lindsey's brigade. Other than normal pickets, the brigade occupied itself unloading material from the boats. Sheldon assigned the 118th Illinois Volunteers the task to guard the Third Division's boats during the operation.[12] While DeCourcy's Brigade fought the enemy without any support, the Third Division leisurely offloaded.

The Fourth Division under Brigadier General Frederick Steele landed adjacent to Johnson's plantation house to the west of Morgan. Also in accordance with Sherman's orders, Steele dispatched Brigadier General Frank P. Blair's First Brigade two miles out on the Vicksburg Road. Blair moved his brigade in column with the 13th Illinois Volunteer Regiment as advance skirmishers and a company of the Tenth Regiment Missouri Cavalry screening his flanks. The 13th Illinois engaged Confederate pickets or patrols and handily pushed them back. Establishing security picketing for the night, Blair bivouacked his brigade.[13] While Blair pushed his brigade forward, Steele ordered his two remaining brigades, the Second under Brigadier General Charles E. Hovey and the Third under Brigadier John M. Thayer to unload the boats and bivouac near the plantation house.[14]

Brigadier General M. L. Smith's Second Division landed in the afternoon of the 26th just to the west of Steele's Fourth Division. Smith ordered Brigadier General David Stuart to advance his Fourth Brigade along the Vicksburg Road and occupy a position on the western flank of Blair's Brigade. Against no opposition Stuart quickly executed his orders. M. L. Smith directed Colonel Giles A. Smith to unload the boats, bivouac, and allow his tired brigade to recover from their railroad destruction mission at Young's Point the night before.[15]

By late afternoon of the 26th, with most of his army firmly ashore and a better idea of the terrain, Sherman issued his orders for the conduct of battle for the 27th. Sherman directed a general attack along the whole front of his army. Morgan's Third Division was to move southeast, skirting around Chickasaw Bayou through Mrs. Lake's plantation. On this axis Morgan was to take the bridging materials and pontoon train and "effect a secure lodgement on the high ground east of the crossing place."[16] Sherman directed Steele to move to the left, maintaining contact with Morgan, but to cross the bayou at or near Morgan by a seperate causeway or bridge. Once across, Steele was to assault the highground. M. L. Smith's division was to oblique to his left, maintain contact with Steele, and cross the bayou next to Steele's crossing site. Smith was then to seize his section of the highground. Expecting A. J. Smith's division to arrive at any time, Sherman planned for Smith's First Division to move on Vicksburg directly along the Vicksburg Road, clear the obstacles, and "occupy the attention of the battery that stands on the first hill north of Vicksburg."[17] Of all the divisions in the assault, only the First Division was not required to assault the bluffs.

Sherman directed each division to take all required digging tools and to advance with strong skirmishers. Sherman was particularly concerned that the main columns of the divisions must protect against Confederate artillery "in which arm alone is our enemy supposed to be superior to us."[18] In his special instructions Sherman specified that artillery, ambulances, and ammunition wagons alone would accompany the columns and that each division must leave a regiment to guard the boats. In the course of the battle, the availability of pontoons at the proper time, in the nroper quantity would become an issue. This special instruction limiting what the divisions could carry may have served to confuse Third Division subordinates as to who was required to bring bridging material. As will be seen, they did not carry the bridging as directed. Finally, Sherman directed the general assault to begin at 7:00 A.M. and placed his headquarters with M. L. Smith's Second Division.[19]

Clearly there was no sense of urgency in pressing the attack on the 26th. Having landed three divisions just five miles from the main enemy defenses, Sherman allowed the main body of the force to bivouac in the immediate vicinity of the landing sites. The Confederate forces arrayed against him were only two regiments at Mrs. Lake's plantation. This force repelled DeCourcy's attack with only one section of artillery because DeCourcy advanced with no cavalry scouts or supporting artillery. DeCourcy met the only real opposition of the three Union brigades that advanced on the 26th, yet he received no support from the remainder of the Third Division. This leisurely advance against an almost unprepared enemy would cost Sherman in the days ahead.

UNION ADVANCE - 27 DECEMBER

During the night of the 26th into the 27th the winter rains began in earnest. Having embarked in an area normally flooded at this time of the year, the rains concerned Sherman. By the early morning of the 27th, A. J. Smith's First Division had not arrived and Sherman decided to initiate a new plan for the 27th. In consultation with Steele and Porter, Sherman decided to shift forces to the east side of Chickasaw Bayou. Sherman had identified a new approach on that side of the bayou which would allow him to attack with all of his divisions while he waited for A. J. Smith's arrival. He directed Steele to leave Blair's First Brigade in position on the Vicksburg Road to move in conjunction with Morgan's assault. With the remainder of the Fourth Division, Steele was to move upriver and land on a "good levee back from the Yazoo River along the Chickasaw bayou".[20]

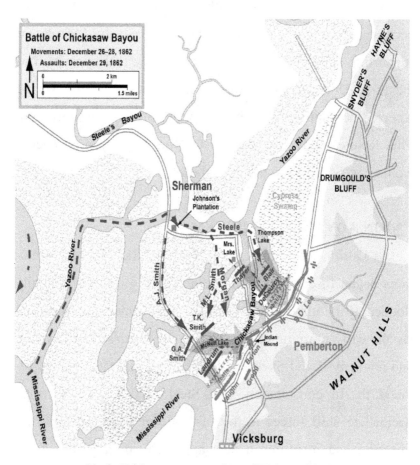

Map by Hal Jespersen, www.posix.com/CW from Wikipedia

Sherman advised Steele to advance along the levee to the bluff keeping near and abreast of Morgan, joining with him as quickly as possible. Sherman still harbored a desire to force the assault at Snyder's Bluff and directed Porter, in addition to supporting Steele's movement, to make a feint on Snyder's Bluff with the object of clearing the river of all torpedoes. Steele was to provide a force to move up the Yazoo on the bank to support the feint by rooting out the Confederates who controlled the command detonated torpedoes.[21] As a result of this conference, Porter directed Lieutenant Commander Gwin to send two gunboats to clear a path for Steele's force and then to shell Snyder's Bluff.[22] Sherman's order shows he had fairly good information on the terrain by his knowledge of the levee on the east side of Chickasaw Bayou. Unfortunately, he did not know that Thompson Lake was between Chickasaw Bayou and the levee, thus a juncture of Steele's and Morgan's divisions would be impossible.

In the early morning of the 27th, Steele detached Blair's Brigade, reloaded his Second and Third Brigades and at 8:00 A.M. began the movement upriver. Slowed by the naval torpedo clearing, Steele arrived at a point between Chickasaw Bayou and Thompson Lake at about noon. Steele's division immediately began the laborious process of cutting a road through the timber to reach the levee.[23]

After covering the landing of Steele's division, Lieutenant Commander Gwin continued upriver with the Benton, De Kalb, Cincinnati, Louisville, Queen of the West, Marmora, and Lexington.[24] As the ironclads crept upriver cautiously searching for torpedoes, heavy gunfire from a force of about four hundred Confederates positioned on the west side of the Yazoo stopped the movement. In response to Porter's request for assistance, Steele dispatched the 17th Missouri Infantry across the Yazoo. The 17th quickly routed the enemy force and returned.[25] The naval force reached a point about three quarters of a mile from Snyder's Bluff, near the wreck of the Cairo, by 3:00 P.M.. By 3:35 P.M. the Confederates at Snyder's Bluff initiated firing on the gunboats. In the duel lasting an hour and thirty five minutes, the gunboats lobbed shell after shell in the hope of diverting Confederate attention. In the process, Gwin was mortally wounded by a rifle shot to his chest and eleven men were wounded.[26] The 22d Louisiana Infantry manning the guns at Snyder's bluff scored twenty four cannon hits on the Union boats, suffering only one killed and two wounded.[27] At about 5:00 P.M. the gunboats withdrew.

Steele's division probably had the first indication of any of Sherman's army as to what difficulties would have to be overcome to get to the bluffs. After corduroying a road through the dry swamp to the levee, Steele found that the levee did not follow the path Sherman had counted on for the battle. Nonetheless, he slowly pushed forward with Hovey's Second Brigade in the lead impeded by heavy timber abatis along the levee. Hovey initially left his 12th Missouri Infantry at the river to guard the boats ordering them forward later that day.[28] Steele's division was terribly exposed on the levee. The levee was well above the surrounding countryside and designed only wide enough to accommodate a wagon. By nightfall, Hovey's brigade had reached the southern end of Thompson Lake where it engaged a small Confederate outpost manned by a company of the 26th Louisiana and a section of 12 pounder cannons from Company A, First Mississippi Light Artillery. After a brief engagement the Confederates withdrew and Steele bivouacked along the levee.[29]

As Steele reembarked on his new mission, Morgan's Third Division began it's advance. DeCourcy lead the attack with the 16th Ohio, 22d Kentucky, 42d Ohio, and 44th Indiana Infantry Regiments. Following in support was Captain Jacob T. Foster's First Wisconsin Battery.[30] Following thirty minutes behind DeCourcy was Lindsey's Second Brigade, and then the 69th Indiana and 120th Ohio Regiments of Sheldon's First Brigade. Sheldon had left the 118th Illinois at the Yazoo to guard the boats. As the Third Brigade advanced on the Lake plantation cotton gin, Colonel Withers advanced the 17th

Louisiana with a howitzer to that position to stop the assault.[31]

As Morgan advanced DeCourcy's Brigade against the cotton gin, Blair moved east from the Vicksburg Road, following a country road leading towards Mrs. Lake's. Blair's mission was to establish contact with DeCourcy's flank and support the Third Division's assault. Blair's approach caused him to broach the woods immediately to the west of Mrs. Lake's house at about noon.[32] Withers was in a tough spot with his small force under heavy attack from two directions. Blair's attack threatened to cut his unit in half. Blair's brigade easily pushed the two companies of the 46th Mississippi stationed in the wood line towards Mrs. Lake's small white house. Withers quickly moved another of Wofford's howitzers in position to support the hard pressed men of the 46th Mississippi and an artillery duel ensued. Under the cover cf the artillery fire on his flank, Withers withdrew the 17th Louisiana to a position in the woods about a half mile south of the plantation house adjacent to the bayou.[33] Captain Louis Hoffman moved his entire 4th Ohio Battery in front of Blair's Brigade and after firing 80 cannon balls, forced the Confederate howitzer with the remnants of the 46th Mississippi companies to retire to the safety of Colonel Withers's new position.[34] Withers ordered two companies of the 26th Louisiana to cross to the east side of the Chickasaw Bayou, take position in the timber and brush along the bank, and to fire on "the abolitionists" as they crept forward.[35]

DeCourcy reached Mrs. Lake's house about 3:00 P.M. where he positioned Foster's battery to support his advance. Continuing south, the hidden sharpshooters of the 26th Louisiana swept the advancing Union troops in their left flank with gun fire. DeCourcy changed his front and advanced the 22d Kentucky, 44th Indiana and part of the 42d Ohio towards the bayou to engage the Confederates. The fight continued for several hours, ending only after Foster's battery forced the Confederates of the 26th Louisiana to retreat. With night falling DeCourcy was forced to bivouac his brigade near the Lake house. During the night DeCourcy assigned the 42d Ohio Regiment to dig in his artillery battery.[36] Withers had accomplished a great deal in one day. With little more than two regiments he had held up an entire Union division and had to engage only two brigades of a possible four available to be used against him. DeCourcy's slow pursuit is particularly noteworthy in that in the days fight he had lost only three killed and fourteen wounded.[37]

As Blair's artillery fire engaged Withers's men at Mrs. Lake's house, Blair halted his force to try to establish contact with DeCourcy and reconnoiter to his right or south east with his Company C, 10th Missouri Cavalry. This element returned shortly and told Blair that the enemy was in great strength beyond the bayou.[38]

Shortly after Blair began his engagement, Brigadier General David Stuart arrived on Blair's right flank as the vanguard of M.L. Smith's Second Division. In an open field to the rear of Blair's brigade, Sherman established his headquarters. At that location Blair and M. L. Smith coordinated their plans. M.L. Smith suggested a joint reconnaissance to the right to find and skirmish with the enemy. Blair agreed, though he may have been given no choice as the movement was coordinated in the presence of Sherman who offered no complaint. For the time being Blair was halted in his movement to link up with Morgan and assist the Third Division's attack. M.L. Smith ordered Stuart to provide a regiment. Stuart tasked the 55th Illinois while Blair chose the 58th Chio.[39] The two regiments quickly moved along the trail towards the Indian Mound passing the "star bespangled soldiers" of Sherman's headquarters with the 55th heartily singing "The Battle Cry of Freedom."[40]

As the two regiments moved forward they were forced to cross over a small creek on one log while their horses swam. On the opposite side, about three hundred yards, the first contact was made by the 58th Ohio in the early afternoon. The 58th deployed while the 55th Illinois massed in reserve to its rear.[41]

The Confederate force struck by the 58th Ohio consisted of three companies of the 31st Louisiana which was headquartered at the Indian Mound. Colonel Charles H. Morrison, commander of the 31st Louisiana, had assigned them the mission at 7:00 A.M. to move across the bayou for a distance of four hundred yards in order to protect a party of slaves cutting abatis and entrenching.[42]

Stuart moved the remainder of his brigade behind the 55th Illinois as soon as he heard the firing and received word about the enemy force. Before he could deploy his brigade, the 58th Ohio had forced he retreat of the Confederate skirmishers to their positions behind the bayou at the Indian Mound, and had formed a skirmish line along the freshly cut abatis. The 55th Illinois was feeding companies into the skirmish line of the 58th trying to suppress the heavy gunfire from the 31st Louisiana. Stuart observed that the Confederates had crossed the bayou "at a narrow and difficult ford or pass" where they occupied rifle pits along the levee on the opposite side.[43]

Soldiers of the 58th Ohio and 55th Illinois may have had the first look at the forbidding ridgeline that Sherman had ordered his divisions to assault. What they observed would make the hardest veteran worry and was typical of the terrain each division would traverse. The Union skirmish line was fifty yards away from the bayou. That fifty yards was a maze of fallen timber. One hundred yards beyond the bayou was the first line of Confederate rifle pits. To the rear of these rifle pits was three quarters of a mile of swampy bottom land reaching to the Walnut Hills. Terraced from the bottom at the Valley Road all the way to the top were rifle pits and entrenchments.[44]

By the time Sherman began his general assault on the morning of the 27th, Brigadier General A. J. Smith had picked up the majority of Brigadier General S.G. Burbridge's First Brigade. Leaving the 131st Illinois on the bank opposite Milliken's Bend in order to pick up stragglers, Smith moved the First Division to the Yazoo. Smith arrived at his landing site near Bunch's sawmill about 1:00 P.M. and immediately began the laborious process of disembarking.

The First Division was not completely unloaded until sunset, at which time the 131st Illinois arrived to take up station as boat guards. Smith moved Burbridge's First Brigade with one battery of the 17th Company, Ohio Light Artillery to overtake the rest of the army. Smith stayed with Colonel William J. Landrum's Second Brigade; Company C, 4th Indiana Cavalry; and the Chicago Mercantile Battery, near the landing site for the rest of the night.[45] Groping their way through the dark, Burbridge's brigade followed a road east along the Yazoo, eventually striking the Johnson's plantation. From the plantation, Burbridge moved along the Vicksburg Road arriving at the country road leading east to Mrs. Lake's plantation at midnight. With gunfire erupting along the bayou to the southeast and towards Mrs. Lake's, Burbridge bivouacked his brigade.[46]

THE CONFEDERATES REINFORCE

During the night of the 27th, the first Confederate reinforcements directed to Vicksburg by Pemberton began to arrive. Brigadier General John C. Vaughn and Brigadier General John Gregg's Brigades arrived from Grenada while Brigadier General Seth Barton arrived as the leading brigade of Major General Carter L. Stevenson's Division from middle Tennessee.[47]

The arrival and employment of the reinforcements highlights an interesting problem developing in the Confederate command structure. The arrival of Pemberton in Vicksburg on the 26th created some command authority problems that were furthur exacerbated by General Johnston's headquarters being established at Jackson, Mississippi. Under the circumstances, Pemberton should have been seeing to the defense of north central Mississippi, while Johnston concerned himself with theater level issues. On the 27th Pemberton received word from his scouts operating from Grenada that Grant had retreated behind the Tallahatchie River and was thought to be moving to Memphis.[48] With no threat from Grant, both Johnston and Pemberton focused on the battle at Chickasaw Bayou. Johnston needled Pemberton as to the disposition of reinforcements, and Pemberton interfered with M. L. Smith's defensive plans. As the battle progressed the command situation changed several times as new generals arrived and assumed command.

With the arrival of the reinforcements, Major General M. L. Smith took over the titular head of the defenses at the bayou from S. D. Lee. Smith decided on an excellent reinforcing plan that would overcome any command problems that existed from the plethora of generals. As reinforcements arrived, they would be fed into the left side of the defensive line where S.D. Lee had left a gap. Each avenue of approach from the Yazoo would be commanded by a brigade commander. If a brigade needed immediate reinforcement, the brigade to its left would provide the necessary troops. In this manner, the regiments would be shifted from the least likely avenue on the left of the Confederate line to the right as the need arose. Smith relied on the cooperation of the brigade commanders and on the skill of the Confederate forces to form and reform brigades as the situation required.[49]

Smith assigned Vaughn's East Tennessee Brigade to the extreme left of the defensive line at the race course. Vaughn deployed the 61st Tennessee Infantry as skirmishers along the bayou while the 60th and 62d Tennessee Infantry Regiments remained in reserve along the high ground to their rear.[50] Barton's Brigade was positioned by Smith at the Indian Mound. Barton found on his arrival that the 31st Louisiana was in position at the mound, and that Vaughn's 62d Tennessee had positioned itself, in the darkness, in support along the Valley Road to the rear of the Louisianans. Barton positioned his Georgians along the hills behind the Valley Road. Smith positioned Gregg's Brigade in reserve. With the addition of these new units, Lee was assigned the defensive sector from the Confederate center to Snyder's Bluff.[51]

As M. L. Smith moved the newly arrived reinforcements into the line, S. D. Lee took measures to defend against the main Union threat on the right flank. Shortly after dark, Lee sent the 29th Louisiana to relieve Withers's force which had battled all day against DeCourcy and Blair at Mrs. Lake's plantation. The 26th Louisiana was placed on the east side of Chickasaw Bayou in order to prevent the 29th from being flanked. Lee assigned Withers command of all troops defending at Blake's Levee against Steele. Withers moved his force to the high ground opposite the levee and checked the state of the defenses. Withers found that the Union forces were on the levee adjacent to Thompson Lake and occupied positions behind a small pond at the turn of the levee. Just a few yards further southeast where the levee sharply turned to the northeast, one company of the 26th Louisiana and seven companies of the 46th Mississippi were positioned to defend. To augment this thin defense, Withers placed an artillery section from Company A, First Mississippi Light Artillery in position to be able to sweep Steele's troops from the side of the levee near Thompson Lake. Withers emplaced three guns from Company I, First Mississippi Light Artillery along the Valley Road in order to sweep the turn of the levee if the Union forces drove the 46th Mississippi off.[52]

The 27th was a pivotal day in the battle at the bayou. The Confederate forces under S. D. Lee were inadequate to defend all the approaches to the bluff yet they were able to slow the Union advance to a crawl. Along the approach on Blake's Levee, one Confederate company, skillfully using the difficult terrain, delayed Steele's brigade until nightfall. This action enabled Lee to reinforce that position from other positions on his battle line. For another whole day, Withers with a tiny force at Mrs. Lake's plantation, held off two brigades under Blair and DeCourcy. The Union commanders were exhibiting extreme caution and an inability or lack of desire to press the attack against small Confederate forces. With the Confederate reinforcements arriving on the night of the 27th, the Union failure to press the attack would be sorely felt.

THE ATTACK CONTINUES - 28 DECEMBER

During the night of the 27th, Union leaders had the first opportunity to conduct a detailed reconnaissance of the principle areas over which the attack would be made.[53] DeCourcy's hotly contested approach to Mrs. Lake's plantation house proved that the Confederates were arrayed in depth at that crossing point. Little was known about the crossing point opposite the Indian Mound until Brigadier General Stuart conducted a personal reconnaissance after dark. He found that the ford had been obstructed by felled timbers which augmented the steep banks up to twenty feet high on the opposite side. Stuart found a narrow path through the tangle, wide enough for only two soldiers to pass side by side. Just to the left of the path the Confederates had heavily manned rifle pits and a battery in control of all approaches to the ford. Stuart had no other choice but to try to clear a larger path. During the night the 116th Illinois worked to clear a path to the ford.[54]

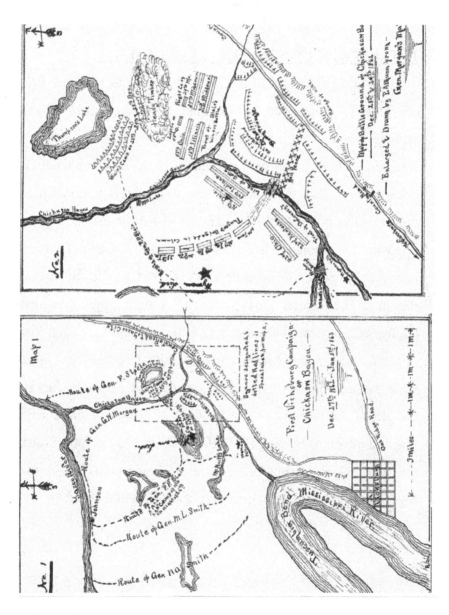

From *History of the Thirteenth Regiment Illinois Volunteer Infantry*, prepared by a committee of the regiment, 1891

118

Though discouraged by the reports detailing the natural formidability of the terrain and the man made obstacles, Sherman did not alter his original plans issued on the 26th.

As dawn approached, Rear Admiral David Porter developed plans to try to assist Sherman in any way possible. True to his character, Porter did not wait for requests for assistance but recommended and implemented operations as he saw fit. At dawn Porter sent the <u>Marmora</u> and <u>Forest Rose</u> up the Old River to fire on Vicksburg to harass the enemy and to assist A. J. Smith's advance if possible. Simultaneously Porter sent mortar boats to shell Steele's left flank and dispatched a small flotilla to shell Snyder's Bluff in order to prevent the Confederates from taking troops from there. Porter continued to wrestle with the problem of getting his boats up the Yazoo with the large number of torpedoes still in the channel. On the 28th, Colonel Ellet of the Ram fleet submitted a plan to Porter to build a special raft, or prow, on the front of a steamer which would act as a rake against the torpedoes. If this system worked, it would allow Porter the ability to move more boats upriver and would offer new tactical flexibility for Sherman. Porter approved the plan.[55]

The morning light of the 28th was obscured by a very heavy layer of fog. As Steele's division uncoiled itself to continue the attack, the fog shielded them from Confederate observation. Hovey as the lead brigade, moved in a column between the levee and Thompson Lake with the 17th Missouri deployed forward as skirmishers. After a short movement of about one quarter mile, the 17th Missouri struck the rifle pits of the 46th Mississippi at the bend in the levee and became pinned down on both sides of the levee. The 46th Mississippi were positioned so that Hovey could not attack them without attacking straight along the levee which was heavily obstructed with timber. The pond at the turn in the levee prevented a cross country approach to the Confederates and the distance between the lake and the levee was wide enough for only a section of infantry (a section was six files or people).[56] Hovey sent a six to eight man pioneer section onto the levee to try to move the obstacles or cut a path with axes. These brave men drew the fire of the 46th Mississippi and from the guns of Company A, First Mississippi Light Artillery. Well aimed cannon fire killed or wounded all the pioneers. As the pioneers made their futile attempt at the levee, the 17th Missouri and Company F, 2d Missouri Light Artillery were trying to dislodge the Confederates in the rifle pits. Continuous attacks failed to dislodge the defenders at the levee. Withers instructed his artillery to stop firing in order to conserve ammunition. Convinced that the Confederate Artillery had been destroyed, Steele decided to mass Hovey's and Thayer's Brigades in the woods between the levee and Thompson Lake. Sending skirmishers forward, Steele advanced his main body in a column about a section wide; he had no other choice. Withers observed the Union troops massing for the assault and quickly got his guns back in action. With heavy cannonading and rifle fire, Steele's skirmishers were repelled time and again. The column of densely packed troops advanced only once before being struck by the cross fire of rebel artillery, halting the attack. It became obvious to Steele that further attempts would be fruitless so he decided to stop and hold his position. Steele brought forward from Thayer's Brigade the 1st Company, Iowa Light Artillery which assisted in the cannon duel.[57] By 4 P.M. Steele had reported his situation to Sherman and received new orders. Steele was to reembark on his boats, move west of Chickasaw Bayou, offload and support Morgan. During the night, Steele carefully disengaged his division in the face of the enemy and moved with Thayer's brigade to Johnson's plantation where it bivouacked. Hovey's brigade had covered the withdrawal and did not move and get on its boats until early morning of the 29th. With little darkness left Hovey's brigade disembarked from the steamers just west of Chickasaw Bayou and bivouacked.[58]

Early in the morning on the 28th the Third Division prepared its assault along Chickasaw Bayou. Morgan ordered the 7th Battery, Michigan Light Artillery, previously attached to the Second Brigade, to move forward and support DeCourcy. DeCourcy positioned the battery adjacent to the south side of the road along the bayou. The battery started receiving fire almost immediately and engaged the 29th Louisiana at its forward road block until almost 9 A.M.. As the Michigan battery was moving into position, DeCourcy's 1st Battery, Wisconsin Light Artillery moved into the earthwork nicknamed "Fort Morgan" by the 42d Ohio which had built it the previous night.[59]

Morgan positioned the rest of the Third Division to begin the general assault by 10:00 P.M.. DeCourcy's Brigade would advance on the axis of the road and bear the brunt of the fight to remove the 29th Louisiana from its position, with the ultimate objective still to seize the highground. Sheldon moved his two regiments to support DeCourcy's left flank. He positioned the 69th Indiana at Mrs. Lake's house and the 120th Ohio next to the bayou. Lindsey was assigned to protect and support DeCourcy on the right flank. Lindsey moved his brigade within easy supporting distance on that flank and put out a strong line of skirmishers. By 10:00 A.M., DeCourcy's canonade and rifle fire appeared to have driven the advanced line of Confederates from their positions so DeCourcy advanced his brigade. DeCourcy found that the Confederates had not given up the fight and immediately requested support from Lindsey. Lindsey moved his 7th Kentucky to the right flank of DeCourcy's Brigade. The ensuing battle lasted several hours in see-saw fighting. As DeCourcy advanced and pressed the 29th Louisiana rearward, Morgan ordered Lindsey to send three companies of skirmishers into the woods across the Chickasaw Bayou to protect that flank. Lindsey moved five companies of the 49th Indiana and within a short time dispatched the five remaining companies due to the heavy fighting on that side. This movement of troops is somewhat strange in that Sheldon was already in position at that flank and the movement of the 49th necessitated crossing laterally through the division.[60]

By noon, DeCourcy had not dislodged the 29th Louisiana. The 29th had counterattacked twice and stymied the attack. Morgan ordered his remaining regiments into action. Morgan ordered Sheldon's 120th Ohio to cross the Bayou and take position to support the 49th Indiana. Sheldon moved the 69th Indiana on DeCourcy's left flank, just to the right of the bayou and then crossed the bayou himself to take command of the division's left flank. Morgan directed Sheldon to make a strong demonstration to distract the Confederates while DeCourcy continued the main attack.[61]

As Sheldon moved his troops across the bayou, and

Morgan pressed his attack against the 29th Louisiana, Colonel Allen Thomas, commander of the 29th, received permission to withdraw from his exposed position. With pressure from both flanks, it became imperative as he withdrew that the 26th Louisiana successfully hold its position. Fortunately for the Confederates, Union mistakes would assist them. Sheldon had moved over the bayou so quickly that he had not brought his staff over with him. As a result he had personally to issue and supervise his orders. His first action was to push a line of skirmishers forward, and follow with the 49th Indiana paralleling the bayou. As the 49th advanced, the commander of the green 120th Ohio, Colonel Daniel French, under orders from a divisional staff officer, moved up to the left flank of the 49th. This premature action caused the 120th to be deployed in a narrow area overrun with log obstacles. In its baptism of fire the 120th became confused and disorganized. With some effort and loss of time, Sheldon was able to sort them out and continued the advance with the two regiments abreast.[62]

Although the timing of the fight is not clear, the 29th Louisiana successfully withdrew by 12:30 P.M.. DeCourcy must have struck the woodline just short of the abatis and main bayou in front of Walnut Hills shortly thereafter. As he made his advance on the bayou Lindsey's regiments on his right flank were struck by artillery fire from the enemy works and enemy skirmishers. Lindsey cleared the woods of the enemy with his 7th Kentucky followed closely by the 114th Ohio. Lindsey's brigade must have reached the bayou at roughly the same time as DeCourcy. Sheldon's brigade forced the 26th out of its positions in a thirty minute fight after the 29th Louisiana had withdrawn. Sheldon probably reached the bayou facing Walnut Hills an hour or so after DeCourcy.[63]

Now the inexplicable happened. Almost the entire Third Division was along the bayou facing Walnut Hills by early to mid afternoon. Sheldon had expected and understood that DeCourcy was to continue the attack. DeCourcy did nothing more than advance his artillery to a forward position along the bayou near the center of his position and begin a cannonade against the Confederate artillery. When Sheldon saw that no attack was to be made, he "did not deem it advisable to do so unsupported" and, after forty five minutes exposed along the bayou, withdrew to cover.[64] In the days fight Sheldon had lost nine killed and fifty three wounded while DeCourcy had ninety five casualties.[65] By Civil War standards these were miniscule losses and certainly were no reason not to continue the assault as planned. There is no evidence that Morgan or Sherman intervened at any time in the afternoon to press the attack. Until nightfall, the Third Division skirmished from cover behind the abatis with Confederate soldiers in rifle pits beyond the bayou.

Blair's First Brigade, Fourth Division was placed in reserve on the morning of the 28th. Between 10 or 11:00 A.M. Sherman ordered Blair to move forward between Morgan and M. L. Smith's Divisions, tying into Smith's left flank. The fight at Mrs. Lake's was becoming intense at this time and Sherman ordered Blair to attach his artillery to the Third Division. Blair dispatched Captain Hoffman's Ohio Battery where it remained for the rest of the day on the right flank of the Third Division. Blair's Brigade advanced to the edge of the bayou and engaged the Confederates in the rifle pits. In the ensuing fight the commander of the 13th Illinois was shot dead. Shortly after noon the fight at Mrs. Lake's plantation and east of the Chickasaw Bayou was at its height. Sherman ordered Blair to shift his brigade to Mrs. Lake's and support the Third Division. Morgan ordered Blair to advance his brigade to the right of the center of the Third Division, probably meaning between DeCourcy and Lindsey. Leading with his 13th Illinois, Blair soon found himself under terrible shell fire not only from enemy batteries, but also friendly artillery. Under these conditions Blair gained Morgan's permission to withdraw the 13th. Morgan then ordered Blair to move his brigade across the bayou where Sheldon was battling the 26th Louisiana. By the time Blair's brigade reached the woodline sheltering Sheldon's brigade, darkness had closed in. After being relieved by Blair,

Sheldon's brigade moved out of its position after dark and moved to the right of Lindsey's brigade.[66]

Brigadier General Stuart's working party of the 116th Illinois was still trying to clear obstructions from the road leading to the ford at 4:30 A.M. on the 28th. With dawn approaching, Stuart ordered the Chicago Mercantile Battery and sharpshooters along the bayou to suppress the rifle pits manned by the 31st Louisiana near the Indian Mound. By dawn Stuart was convinced that he could not clear the obstructions at the foot of the hill near the bayou. He reported this to Sherman who directed Stuart to keep the enemy occupied and try to cross the bayou simultaneously with Morgan. Stuart reported these new instructions to M. L. Smith who decided to take a look himself.[67] M. L. Smith and an orderly rode to the most advanced positions held by Stuart's men. Brushing aside warnings from the sheltered riflemen, Smith rode to a most exposed position to observe the Confederate position. Shortly he reigned his horse, passed the soldiers issuing "pungent and profane instructions", and after leaving the forward troop area fell from his horse. Smith had been severely wounded as he scrutinized the enemy positions.[68] Sherman ordered Stuart at 8:00 A.M. to assume temporary command of the Second Division.

The Confederate position at the Indian Mound under

Brigadier General Barton became the center of reinforcement activity during the 28th. Although heavily engaged at the Indian Mound, Barton was perfectly positioned to coordinate the shifting of troops along the battle line using the Valley Road. Early in the day, S. D. Lee requested additional support to back up his Louisianans fighting Morgan's division. Barton coordinated with Vaughn to move the 62d Tennessee from their positions behind the 31st Louisiana at the Indian Mound to the high ground at Lee's position. Barton replaced the 62d Tennessee with the 40th Georgia. In the early afternoon when Morgan pressed the 29th and 26th Louisiana Regiments across the bayou, Barton shifted his 42d Georgia to Lee's left flank, opposite Blair's early morning position on the bayou. Barton drew the 3d Tennessee from Gregg's reserve brigade to fill the gap left by the 42d. The Confederate plan to introduce troops from left to right was working well.[69]

As Stuart took command he observed the shifting of the Confederate forces at the Indian Mound. He concluded that the enemy was reinforcing the position and ordered up the First Brigade under Brigadier General Giles Smith to support the Fourth Brigade now commanded by Colonel T. Kilby Smith. Stuart ordered Kilby Smith to clear the obstructions on the road and get into position to attack. Kilby Smith immediately deployed his batteries of the First Illinois Light Artillery on the left of the road and augmented the skirmishers along the bayou. As work progressed into the late morning, the entire 55th Illinois was pressed into service along the abatis to try to suppress the Confederates at the Indian Mound. The fire against the 31st Louisiana became so severe that Barton had to move 100 men of the 40th Georgia into the rifle pits to reinforce that position. In the early afternoon Sherman ordered Stuart to cross the bayou because Morgan was in the process of crossing. Stuart ordered the Fourth Brigade to attack. By 3:00 P.M. Kilby Smith had his 54th Ohio in the road ready to attack across the still obstructed ford site. Just as the attack was to be ordered, Brigadier General A. J. Smith rode up to assume command of the Second Division under Sherman's orders. Stuart apprised Smith of the dire situation and recommended that the attack be called off as impossible. Smith temporarily suspended the attack as it was clear that the Third Division had also not attacked. Smith ordered that work continue to clear the obstructions. For the remainder of the day the 54th Ohio labored under terrible fire to remove the obstacles.[70] By dusk Stuart pulled the 54th Ohio back from its dangerous work and the Second Division bivouacked as best as could be managed so close to the enemy.

The 28th was a relatively quiet day for A. J. Smith's First Division. Very early in the morning Smith left his landing site at the Yazoo to catch up with Burbridge's brigade and the rest of the army. By 8:00 A.M. Smith arrived at the army's camp ground of the previous night with Colonel Landrum's Second Brigade and his artillery. Sherman ordered Smith to position Burbridge's First Brigade with his battery of the Ohio Light Artillery on the right flank of the Second Division. Landrum's Second Brigade with the Chicago Mercantile Battery and with Company C, 4th Indiana Cavalry was to occupy a position at the junction of the roads leading to Vicksburg and recon toward the city.[71]

This intersection was probably the fork off the Vicksburg Road leading to Mrs. Lake's. Burbridge's brigade did nothing more during the day except build rafts to use to cross McNutt Lake. Landrum sent several patrols towards the race course and engaged pickets from the 61st Tennessee which were posted on the north side of the bayou.[72] At 3:00 P.M. A. J. Smith took command of the Second Division also. With the minute activity his division was tasked to perform, he certainly wasn't challenged by the added responsibility.

Another day of lost opportunity passed for the Union. The Confederates had by now discerned the exact plan of attack of the Union army by the obvious array of forces to their front. The Union pause in the attack on the bluffs in the afternoon of the 28th allowed the Confederates to skillfully shift the available reinforcements along the most likely Union axes of attack. Again the Confederates had been able to stop the overwhelming Union forces far forward of their main defensive line using a mere fraction of their available regiments.

ENDNOTES

1. Thomas B. Marshall, History of the Eighty Third Ohio Volunteer Infantry (Cincinnati: The Eighty Third Ohio Vol. Infantry Association, 1913), 53.

2. Stephen D. Lee, "The Campaign of General Grant and Sherman against Vicksburg in December 1862 and January 1st and 2d, 1863, known as the 'Chickasaw Bayou Campaign' " in Publications of the Mississippi Historical Sociei¬y, Franklin L. Riley, (Oxford, Mississippi: Harrisburg Publishing Co., 1902) IV: 24-25 and William T. Sherman, Memoirs of General W.T. Sherman (New York: The Library of America, 1990), 312-313.

3. The War of Rebellion: A Compilation of the Official Records of the Union and Confederate Armies 128 vols. (Washington: Government Printing Office, 1880-1901) Series I, Vol. XVII, Part 1: 472. (Cited hereafter as OR.) and Lee, "The Campaign," 24-25.

4. Lee, "The Campaign," 24.

5. Ibid., 25.

6. OR, Series I, Vol. XVII, Part 1, 681 and Herman Hattaway,

"Confederate Myth Making: Top Command and the Chickasaw Bayou Campaign," The Journal of Mississippi History 32 (November 1970): 319.

7. OR, Series I, Vol. XVII, Part 1, 637.

8. Ibid., 681.

9. Ibid., 637.

10. Ibid., 686.

11. Ibid., 646.

12. Ibid., 644.

13. Ibid., 651, 653.

14. Edwin C. Bearss, The Campaign for Vicksburg 3 vols. (Dayton, OH: Morningside House, Inc., 1985) 1: 161.

15. OR, Series I, Vol. XVII, Part 1, 634-635 and Bearss, 161.

16. OR, Series I, Vol. XVII, Part 1, 621.

17. Ibid.

18. OR, Series I, Vol. XVII, Part 1, 621.

19. Ibid.

20. OR, Series I, Vol. XVII, Part 2, 878.

21. Ibid.

22. The War of Rebellion: A Compilation of the Official Records of the Union and Confederate Navies, 31 vols. (Washington: Government Printing Office, 1894-1922) series I, Vol. XXIII: 571. (Cited hereafter as ORN).

23. <u>OR</u>, Series I, Vol. XVII, Part 1, 651.

24. <u>ORN</u>, Series I, Vol. XXIII, 573 and Bearss, 164.

25. <u>OR</u>, Series I, Vol. XXII, 651.

26. <u>ORN</u>, Series I, Vol. XXIII, 573,579,675.

27. <u>OR</u>, Series I, Vol. XVII, Part 1, 694.

28. Henry A. Kircher, <u>A German in the Yankee Fatherland - The Civil War Letters of Henry A. Kircher</u> ed. Earl J. Hess, (Kent, OH: Kent State University Press, 1983), 42-43.

29. <u>OR</u>, Series I, Vol. XVII, Part 1, 651 and Bearss, 165-166.

30. <u>OR</u>, Series I, Vol. XVII, Part 1, 642,648.

31. Ibid., 686.

32. <u>OR</u>, Series I, Vol. XVII, Part 1, 654 and Committee of the Regiment, <u>The Story of the Fifty Fifth Regiment Illinois Volunteer Infantry,</u> (Clinton, Mass: W.J. Coulter, 1887), 188.

33. <u>OR</u>, Series I, Vol. XVII, Part 1, 686.

34. Ibid., 646.

35. Ibid., 687.

36. Ibid., 642, 648.

37. Ibid.

38. Ibid., 654.

39. Ibid., 635.

40. <u>The Story of the Fifty Fifth,</u> 189.

41. <u>OR</u>, Series I, Vol. XVII, Part 1, 635 and <u>The Story of the Fifty Fifth,</u> 189.

42. <u>OR</u>, Series I, Vol. XVII, Part 1, 696.

43. Ibid., 635.

44. The Story of the Fifty-Fifth, 190.

45. <u>OR</u>, Series I, Vol. XVII, Part 1, 627.

46. Bearss, 172.

47. <u>OR</u>, Series I, Vol. XVII, Part 1, 666.

48. <u>OR</u>, Series I, Vol. XXII, Part 2, 807.

49. <u>OR</u>, Series I, Vol. XVII, Part 1, 672.

50. <u>OR</u>, Series I, Vol. XVII, Part 1, 678 and Bearss, 224.

51. <u>OR</u>, Series I, Vol. XVII, Part 1, 666, 677.

52. <u>OR</u>, Series I, Vol. XVII, Part 1, 686-687 and Bearss, 185.

53. <u>OR</u>, Series I, Vol. XVII, Part 1, 606.

54. Ibid., 635.

55. <u>ORN</u>, Series I, Vol. XXIII, 578, 581-582, 591.

56. William H.Morris<u>, Infantry Tactics</u>, (New York: D. Van Nostrand, 1865)1: 23.

57. <u>OR</u>, Series I, Vol. XVII, Part 1, 651, 688 and Kircher, 44-45.

58. <u>OR</u>, Series I, Vol. XVII, Part 2, 606, 651 and Kircher, 46.

59. <u>OR</u>, Series I, Vol. XVII, Part 1, 641-642, 645.

60. Ibid., 644, 647, 649, 695-696.

61. Ibid., 644-605.

62. Ibid., 644,681.

63. Ibid., 641, 643, 647.

64. Ibid., 644.

65. Ibid., 645, 649.

66. OR, Series I, Vol. XVII, Part 1, 645-646, 654-655.

67. Ibid., 635.

68. The Story of the Fifty Fifth, 191.

69. OR, Series I, Vol. XVII, Part 1, 677 and Bearss, 184.

70. OR, Series I, Vol. XVII, Part 1, 635-636, 697 and The Story of the Fifty Fifth, 192-193,195.

71. OR, Series I, Vol. XVII, Part 1, 627-628.

72. OR, Series I, Vol. XVII, Part 1, 607 and Bearss, 189-190.

CHAPTER FOUR - THE BATTLE AT CHICKASAW BAYOU

TACTICAL COMBAT OPERATIONS - ATTACK AND REPULSE
29 DECEMBER 1862 - 4 JANUARY 1863

By the evening of the 28th, Sherman supposed that the enemy he faced now numbered 15,000 men. His commanders had observed the movement of Confederate troops on the bluffs and concluded that some reinforcement was occurring.

Sherman had heard nothing from Grant and feared that if Grant and Rosecrans were not occupying Pemberton and Bragg respectively, 4,000 Confederate reinforcements could be expected daily. Sherman concluded that the main attack would have to be executed on the 29th.[1]

ATTACK ON THE BLUFFS-29 DECEMBER

Sherman directed his divisions to attack simultaneously along the entire front. The Third Division was the main attack and would assault across the Valley Road and secure a lodgement at the top of the bluffs. Blair's brigade on the east side of Chickasaw Bayou would follow on the flank of the attack made by the Third Division and support the Third's attack as required. Following behind and in support of Morgan's main attack would be Steele's Fourth Division, the army reserve, with the mission to secure the Valley Road as Morgan crested the bluffs. A.J. Smith was assigned two missions as the commander of the First and Second Divisions. He was to leave one brigade guarding the intersection of the Vicksburg Road and the road to Mrs. Lake's to ensure the Confederates could not flank the army. The First Brigade, First Division under Burbridge was to cross the bayou and secure the Valley Road, orienting on Vicksburg and protecting that flank from counterattack. The Second Division was to attack at the Indian Mound and secure a lodgement on the face of the hill.[2]

The affect of Sherman's orders was to create an attack that would leave the army arrayed in the shape of an arrowhead. Morgan's division was the point on the crest with a solid wall of Union defenders on the flanks angled back down to the bayou and oriented outwards to defend against counterattack. Steele's division in the center would be the force to push up through the tip of the arrowhead and continue the attack of the army.

THE MAIN ATTACK

During the afternoon and evening of the 28th, Morgan had done a reconnaissance of his divisional front. Seven hundred yards west of the corduroy bridge crossing site on the road from Mrs. Lake's, Morgan saw that the Confederates had not defended because McNutt Lake formed an eighty foot wide channel. Morgan felt he could bridge the lake at night and send Lindsey and Sheldon's brigades across to support DeCourcy and Blair's attack along Chickasaw Bayou. With the bridge Morgan would double the number of brigades simultaneously attacking S.D. Lee's stronghold on the bluffs. Unfortunately for the Union Morgan made his first unforgivable mistake of the battle. Sherman had specifically directed Morgan to carry the pontoon train with him after landing on the 26th. For unknown reasons Morgan did not carry them forward and after dark on the 28th had to send his engineer, Captain W. F. Patterson, back to the steamers to pick up eight pontoons. In the darkness Patterson and his engineer mechanics made a terrible mistake and bridged a water slough parallel to the bluff, not McNutt Lake. Morgan discovered the error just before dawn and quickly redirected Patterson to the correct crossing site.[3] At daybreak Morgan and Lindsey found that the enemy had still not reinforced the area opposite the pontoon site so there was still an excellent chance to bridge the site quickly. However,

Patterson advised Morgan that in the haste to leave Memphis army engineers had failed to bring trestles on which to lay planks between the pontoons. Thus he had only forty eight feet of usable bridging. Patterson estimated that he could cut down trees to make rafts and lash them side by side with the pontoons, an operation that would take two hours to accomplish.[4] Morgan's failure to obey his orders had gravely hurt the chances for the attack. Had he obeyed orders on the 26th, his engineers would not have had to make the trip in the dark to obtain bridging and thus bridged at the wrong site. Had the pontoons been brought forward as ordered, Patterson would have already ascertained the pontoon equipment shortfall well before the attack and prepared the necessary bridging improvisations. In his memoirs Morgan would try to shift the blame for this failure onto Sherman for the hasty departure from Memphis. It is clear who was ultimately negligent.

Patterson's bridging operation caught the attention of the Confederates almost immediately. Artillery from Lee's Company D, 1st Mississippi Light Artillery and Company A, 14th Mississippi Light Artillery directed cannon fire against the bridge. Lee then shifted Colonel Allen Thomas with the 42d Georgia and 29th Louisiana opposite bridge site. Thomas initially deployed two companies of the 29th and four companies of the 42d forward along the lake. The remainder of those regiments were placed in reserve. Lee realized that a major battle was developing and ordered the 4th Mississippi Regiment to move from Snyder's Bluff to Chickasaw Bayou. The work of the engineers could not continue under the Confederate fire so Colonel Sheldon moved his 69th Indiana along the bayou to try to suppress Thomas's defenders.[5]

At first light Blair had just started a reconnaissance of his front when the firing against the pontoon site caused Morgan to believe an attack was imminent on the right flank. Morgan ordered Blair to cross back over the bayou and get in position behind DeCourcy to repel the attack. Shortly thereafter Morgan realized the true situation and countermanded the orders allowing Blair to continue his reconnaissance. Moving a battalion of the 13th Illinois out as skirmishers, Blair inspected the ground to his front. He was appalled at the terrain and the Confederate defenses. The Confederate defenses allowed them to enfilade his line from both sides. In the attack his brigade would have to emerge from the timber, try to penetrate a thickly set stand of cottonwoods cut by the Confederates to three feet in height, and descend eight to ten feet into the 100 foot wide bayou. The bayou contained water about fifteen feet wide which was deep and boggy. At the other side of the bayou was another eight to ten foot embankment with abatis and crowned with rifle pits. Just to the rear of the embankment was another string of rifle pits and still furthur back, at the elevated Valley Road, the Confederates had placed their artillery batteries.[6]

Unknown to Blair, S. D. Lee had withdrawn elements of the 26th Louisiana from advanced rifle pits on the Union side of the bayou. Lee wanted nothing to prevent the Union forces from attacking at this point and thereby hitting him frontally. Lee would get his wish.[7]

Early in the morning Steele moved from his landing site at Johnson's plantation with Thayer's brigade. Hovey's brigade was still disembarking near the Chickasaw Bayou so Steele ordered him to move up as soon as possible. Steele met Sherman and Morgan at Mrs. Lake's house and was told to hold his brigade there and be prepared to support the attack of the Third Division. Morgan told Steele that he expected the pontoon bridge to be constructed in two hours and that the attack would commence thirty minutes after that. Morgan requested assistance from Steele to augment the Third Division's assault force. Steel promised him Thayer's brigade immediately and Hovey's when it arrived.[8]

Morgan had concentrated the guns of the 7th Michigan, the 4th Ohio, and the 1st Wisconsin batteries in the field south of Mrs. Lake's. Protecting these batteries Morgan had drawn two regiments from Blair, the 30th and 32d Missouri. These batteries began a terrific cannonade against the Confederate batteries at 7:30 A.M. which continued until 10:00 A.M..[9]

Along S. D. Lee's front, rifle and cannon fire continued well into the morning as Morgan made preparations and waited for his pontoon bridge to be finished. Colonel Withers became convinced that the lack of any activity to his front at Blake's Levee meant the attack would fall on the center of Lee's line. Withers positioned more of his artillery forward so that he could enfilade any attack on the center and made preparations to reinforce Lee with some of his regiments.[10]

By 10:00 A.M. the pontoon bridge still had not been constructed due to the heavy fire against the working party. At this point Morgan and Sherman diverge in their accounts of the interchange between the two concerning the decision to go ahead with the attack. Morgan claimed in his account of the battle, twenty two years after the war, that he had believed an attack across the corduroy bridge by DeCourcy was too dangerous without a simultaneous assault over the pontoon bridge. At Morgan's request Sherman moved forward from his headquarters at Mrs. Lake's house to see personally what Morgan was talking about and after this reconnaissance supposedly stated that "This is the route to take" and rode away without further comment.[11] Shortly thereafter Morgan contends that Sherman sent him a courier with the following verbal instructions: "Tell Morgan to give the signal for the assault; that we will lose 5,000 men before we take Vicksburg, and we may as well lose them here as anywhere else."[12] Sherman reported this exchange much differently in his memoirs. Sherman said that Morgan indicated to Sherman that "General, in ten minutes after you give the signal I'll be on those hills."[13] With that Morgan alerted his brigades to prepare for the attack.

With his 30th and 32d Missouri guarding the artillery, Blair established the remainder of his brigade in two lines of battle 150 feet apart. On the forward left was the 31st Missouri and on the forward right was the 13th Illinois. In the following battle line was the 29th Missouri on the left, the 58th Ohio on the right.[14] When told by Morgan to form his brigade and prepare to assault, DeCourcy exclaimed "My poor brigade! Your order will be obeyed, General."[15] DeCourcy formed his brigade with one line of battle consisting of the 54th Indiana on the left, the 22d Kentucky on the right. Following behind the 54th was the 16th Ohio in double column. Behind the 22d, also in double column, was the 42d Ohio.[15] Morgan ordered Lindsey and Sheldon to continue bridging during the attack and try to cross the bayou over the pontoons or by crossing the bayou further to the west. Morgan had assured Lindsey that two additional regiments from Thayer would be forthcoming. To Steele, Morgan directed that Thayer's brigade was to follow and support DeCourcy's brigade; he did not mention the requirement to send Lindsey two regiments.[17]

The Third Division was ready to attack at 12:00; S. D. Lee was ready to defend. Morgan initiated the attack with another cannonade against the center of Lee's line which prompted Withers to dispatch immediately the 17th and 26th Louisiana regiments with additional artillery to Lee's position.[18] Blair's brigade on the left rushed out of the woods when the cannons fired. Advancing through the terrible obstacles and deluged by rifle fire and enfilading cannon fire the brigade managed to carry the first and second line of rifle pits. The brigade was taking a terrible beating. Looking to the center, Blair could see that DeCourcy had reached the first rifle pits. Encouraged, Blair's brigade continued to battle onward. By the time Blair's brigade reached the last line of entrenchments at the Valley Road, held by the 30th Tennessee Regiment, almost one third of the brigade was down. Blair could not hold his position at the road and ordered a withdrawal. Without panic Blair's troops pulled back and crossed over the bayou at the corduroy bridge over which DeCourcy had attacked.[19]

DeCourcy's movement into the attack immediately was thrown off by the terrain. The 54th Indiana followed by the 16th Ohio and part of the 22d Kentucky had the easiest route over the bayou by following the road over the corduroy bridge.

To their right, the main body of the 22d Kentucky and the 42d Ohio slowly penetrated the abatis only to find they could not wade through the bayou; it was simply too deep. The 54th Indiana and 16th Ohio had immediately deployed into line of battle on the opposite side and had carried the first line of rifle pits. This is what Blair had observed in his attack. DeCourcy ordered the 22d Kentucky and 42d Ohio to move to the left flank, push through the abatis and cross over the bridge in the wake of the 54th and 16th. Unfortunately by the time they broke through and crossed over, the 54th and 16th had attacked unsupported into the heart of the Confederate defenders. They didn't stand a chance and were mowed down in huge numbers in the open ground in front of the Valley Road. Within a short time the Confederates had forced DeCourcy's two lead regiments into retreat. Seeing his advanced elements in retreat, DeCourcy did not wish to destroy any other units. He positioned the 42d Ohio along the bank of the bayou on the opposite side to cover the withdrawal of his mauled brigade.[20]

As the attack commenced Morgan made another costly error that he would later dismiss as a fortunate misunderstanding that ultimately saved lives.[21] It may have saved lives, but it reduced his attack force by an entire brigade. As Thayer lead his brigade forward, Morgan remembered his commitment to Lindsey for two of Thayer's regiments. Morgan approached Steele and requested that he shift a part of Thayer's brigade to the right to support Lindsey. Since Thayer had already moved at the head of the column with the 4th Iowa, Steele intercepted Colonel Charles H. Abbott of the 30th Iowa, second in the order of march, and ordered him to the right. Abbott obeyed and moved off to the right. In this rough terrain with very limited visibility. Thayer had issued a standing order to his units to follow the regiment in front. Steele promptly departed before observing that Thayer's four remaining regiments followed the 30th Iowa on its useless trek to the right. Thayer at the head of the 4th Iowa crossed over the corduroy bridge on the heels of the DeCourcy's brigade. Once across the bayou Thayer ordered Colonel James H. Williamson to move the 4th Iowa to the right and deploy them as advance skirmishers for the brigade. Thayer was so intent on the mission at hand that his force had entered the depths of the Confederate defenses before he turned and saw that the five regiments he had supposed were following him had disappeared. Ordering the 4th Iowa to hold in position, Thayer returned to the corduroy bridge in search of his brigade. Thayer saw the 42d Ohio sheltering along the bayou bank and supposed them to be skulking. Thayer pleaded with the 42d Ohio to come to his assistance but was refused. Having no other choice Thayer returned to the 4th Iowa and while

DeCourcy's brigade fled on the left, ordered the Iowans to hold for thirty minutes while he searched for help. After thirty fruitless minutes, the 4th Iowa pulled back from its exposed forward position. This brave regiment had gone into the battle with 480 men, and during the half hour fight lost 7 killed and 104 wounded.[22]

Morgan would contend that the mistake of shifting Thayer's brigade saved that brigade from destruction. Knowing the Confederate situation in front of the 4th Iowa illustrates that a full brigade may well have carried the day. The attack by the 4th Iowa had been blunted by the timely intervention of Colonel Allen Thomas of the 29th Louisiana. While his skirmishers were occupied with the pontoon bridge, Thomas had been observing the Union assault on Lee's center. Thomas became aware of the success of the 4th Iowa as it rolled up towards Lee's left flank, apparently without much opposition. The enemy to Thomas's front was not putting up much of an attack so Thomas ordered the main elements of the 29th Louisiana and the 42d Georgia to attack towards the 4th Iowa. Without any support the 4th Iowa was compelled to retreat.[23] Had the rest of Thayer's brigade been with the 4th Iowa, the Confederates might have been flanked before Thomas could intervene.

Union failure at the pontoon site also contributed to

Thomas's ability to fight off the 4th Iowa. Lindsey failed to execute the plan as directed by Morgan. Morgan had ordered Lindsey to force a crossing in his area with or without the bridge. The implied task was to find a place and cross during DeCourcy's attack. In order to accomplish this Morgan had placed Sheldon in support of Lindsey. At noon Lindsey had moved his brigade behind the 62d Indiana on the bayou and had redoubled his fire to suppress the Confederate defenders. A hidden battery opened up causing Lindsey to believe his position was untenable. Under this fire and learning of DeCourcy's repulse, Lindsey reported his situation to Morgan and received permission to withdraw.[24] Morgan hints that this attack may not have been very aggressive, particularily when he had ordered Lindsey to force a crossing regardless of the status of the bridge. Thomas certainly was not impressed by Lindsey's assault. He shifted his entire command against the 4th Iowa as Lindsey feebly attacked.

As Thomas battled the 4th Iowa, Lee saw his chance to counterattack DeCourcy's retreating brigade. Lee took the 26th and 17th Louisiana which had just marched from Withers' position and charged them directly onto the battlefield.

The two regiments swept over the field where DeCourcy's men sheltered from the withering fire and captured 21 officers and 311 soldiers. Lee evacuated some of

DeCourcy's wounded but sharp skirmishing prevented many from getting assistance. After observing the battlefield Lee estimated the Union had lost well over 1000 men.[25]

Hovey's Second Brigade caught up with Steele at Mrs. Lake's house as the remnants of DeCourcy's and Blair's brigades reformed and prepared for the expected renewal of the attack. Steele posted Hovey in the same position on the east side of the bayou from which Blair had made his attempt against the heights. Steele reported to Morgan that Hovey's brigade were waiting with great anticipation for the assault. It was not quite so. Lieutenant Henry A. Kircher of the 12th Missouri remembered feeling a terrible dread that "nobody would easily come through alive" upon seeing the route over which they were to charge.[26]

By 3:30 P.M. Morgan was convinced that to continue the attack would be futile and he recommended to Sherman that bridge work discontinue and the attack be suspended. Morgan also wanted to send out a flag of truce to bring in the wounded and bury the dead. Sherman agreed to a cessation of the attack but initially refused to ask for a truce. At dusk Sherman relented but in the dark the Confederates fired on the truce party and Morgan called off the effort. Morgan's heavily reinforced division had suffered 154 killed, 757 wounded, and 528 missing in the day's fight.[27]

ATTACK AT THE INDIAN MOUND

Brigadier General Stuart's Fourth Brigade had borne the brunt of the skirmishing and obstacle destruction during the Second Division's advance to the bayou. Early in the morning of the 29th, A. J. Smith ordered Colonel Giles Smith to relieve the Fourth Brigade with his First Brigade. A. J. Smith ordered Giles Smith to force a crossing and gain the hills on the opposite side. Stuart's Brigade was to follow closely behind his assault while Burbridge's First Brigade, First Division was to support by fire from along the bayou to the west. Landrum's Brigade was to make a demonstration along the Vicksburg Road towards the race course.[28]

Stuart left the 57th Ohio along the west side of the path leading to the bayou to support Giles Smith. Giles Smith moved his 13th U.S. Infantry to the east side of the path and ordered both units to suppress the Confederates during the preparation and assault. These regiments, with artillery support, moved into position under a furious fire against Barton's position at the Indian Mound lasting until 7:00 A.M. Smith could see that there was no open crossing site on the opposite bank. Clearly this would have to be improved before he could hope to move a regiment across. Smith ordered one company of the 6th Missouri with a working party of twenty engineer mechanics to cross and construct a road through the bank. Once

150

this was done, the 6th Missouri led by Lieutenant Colonel James H. Blood was to cross and gain a lodgement. The 8th Missouri would follow with the 116th Illinois and finally the 13th U.S. Infantry.[29]

The signal to attack was to be the artillery preparation from Morgan's division. By noon A. J. Smith's two divisions were prepared to assault. Landrum had closed on the race course and had initiated skirmishing. The obstacles at that position were so formidable that any thought of approach through them was not considered by A. J. Smith. Burbridge's brigade was arrayed along the bayou to the west of Giles Smith. Giles Smith was positioned at the ford site with his storming party of riflemen and engineers. About noon Morgan's artillery thundered and Smith's assault party charged across the bayou. This force quickly realized that the task was too formidable and began to try to dig through the bank so as to allow the troops an access through. Under heavy fire, Giles Smith found a small path to the left of the working party through which two men abreast might get to the top. Smith decided that he had to try to use this path as well as the path being cut, so he ordered the 6th Missouri to cross. The advanced rifle pits of the 31st Lousiana were literally on top of the bank. The 6th Missouri sheltered underneath the bank waiting for the engineers to finish breaching. As rifle and shell fire swept downwards, the 6th

Missouri burrowed into the embankment to protect themselves.[30]

Barton reinforced the hard pressed 31st Louisiana with the 52d Georgia and four guns of Battery A, 1st Mississippi Light Artillery very early in the fight. Five times that afternoon Barton sustained attacks to overcome the parapet each time his force held the Union troops away. The pressure was so great that late in the day Barton requested reinforcements and Vaughn responded by sending his 60th Tennessee.[31]

As the battle of the Indian Mound was being fought, the misdirected regiments of Thayer's brigade arrived on the left flank of the 13th U.S. Infantry. Colonel Abbott of the 30th Iowa realized that he was completely off the mark having joined with the Second Division rather than Lindsey's brigade of the Third Division. Receiving fire from the direction of the Indian Mound, Abbott had his troops lay down and sent a runner to Steele for instructions. In the late afternoon Steele ordered him back and he linked up with Thayer before dark at Mrs. Lake's house.[32]

Giles Smith became convinced that to try to charge into the Confederate defenses through the narrow path was suicidal. As it was the men of the 6th Missouri were so close to the 31st Louisiana that their rifle barrels and bayonets touched as the 31st reached over the bank to shoot downwards. Confederate soldiers even threw corn bread down to the besieged Union soldiers.[33] Just before dark, Smith positioned the 8th Missouri along the bayou to add rifles to the skirmish line and under the combined fire of three regiments the 6th Missouri recrossed the bayou.[34]

The Union forces attacking on the 29th faced one of the most difficult tactical challenges ever encountered in the Civil War. The attack was bravely executed by the soldiers, but miserably controlled by the generals. The focal point of the attack that day was the Third Division.

The Third Division had the best route over which to attack and had four brigades with an additional brigade in support. Directly as a result of command failures by General Morgan in failing to carry the pontoon bridge and the redirecting of Thayer's brigade, only one of his four brigades ever stormed the Confederate works.

DEVELOPING A NEW PLAN

Sherman's main attack on the bluffs had failed and during the night of the 29th Sherman ordered his divisions to prepare to renew the attack on the 30th. Another freezing cold rain that night, the whistling trains signalling the arrival of Confederate reinforcements, and the total communications blackout with Grant added to Sherman's concerns. Early on the

30th Sherman rode along the battle line and became convinced that another attack was futile. Under the circumstances, he felt he could still posture himself on the Yazoo to link with Grant who he felt certain must be coming soon. He issued instructions to his commanders to pull back out of rifle range and rest the troops. The army was ordered to dig in the artillery, build corduroy roads to assist in resupply, and to save ammunition by not replying to enemy fire.[3]

The Confederates used the respite on the 30th to make the final command reorganization along the Walnut Hills. Major General Carter L. Stevenson arrived with the lead elements of Brigadier General Edward D. Tracy's brigade to take command of his division, of which Barton's and Vaughn's had arrived at the battlefield. As the ranking major general, Stevenson took command of the entire line of battle from Major General M. L. Smith. Late in the afternoon Major General Dabney H. Maury arrived from Grenada with a small portion of his division. The rest of his division was strung out from Vicksburg to Grenada on the railroad. An informal arrangement was worked out between Maury and Stevenson whereby Stevenson directly commanded the front where Vaughn, Barton and Gregg were positioned and Maury took the rest of the front all the way to Snyder's Bluff. Other than returning skirmishing fire, the Confederates were not pressured in any way.[36]

In close consultation with Porter, Sherman developed a new scheme to get at the Confederates. Porter advised Sherman that he now had the capability to clear the Yazoo channel using the rake Colonel Ellet had experimented with since the 28th. Sherman directed Steele's Fourth Division to be ready to embark on the expedition at nightfall. He ordered one brigade of the Second Division to be attached to Steele. A. J. Smith selected Giles Smith's First Brigade. Sherman cautioned the commanders to be very careful to screen their movement to the Yazoo from the Confederates. The rest of the army was given the warning to be prepared for instant action to support the new attack.[37]

Sherman and Porter's plan required the ram Lioness to clear ahead of the convoy using the new rake with four gunboats following. The troop transports would then follow and the remainder of the gunboats would guard the rear. Porter had developed good intelligence on the area from escaped slaves from the Johnson, Lake, and Blake plantations. Porter convinced Sherman that, like the area at the bayou, the only way to get at Snyder's Bluff was to cruise upriver and disembark the soldiers in the face of the enemy at Skillet Goliah Bayou.[38]

At dark, Steele and Giles Smith skillfully withdrew their soldiers to the Yazoo.[39] By midnight everything was ready for the upriver movement. Sherman left the river and moved back to his headquarters at Mrs. Lake's anticipating a 4:00 A.M. assault. The remainder of the army would conduct a large scale demonstration along the entire front to draw Confederate attention. At dawn Sherman received a bitterly disappointing note from Steele. Porter could not move upriver because of the fog and the expedition would have to be delayed twenty four hours.[40]

The battle line was quiet on the 31st. Morgan sent out a flag of truce about 11:00 A.M. and obtained permission to bring in the wounded and bury the dead.[41] Late in the afternoon Porter advised Sherman that with moon set at 5:05 A.M. on 1 January, the attack would be as illuminated as if they attacked during daylight. This was simply too dangerous to attempt. Sherman had to assess his chances again. Weighing heavily on his mind was the ground he occupied. The winter rains had commenced in earnest and he could tell from the water rings on the trees above his head that he was in a dangerous place. He was now convinced from rumors coming downriver that the Confederates were reinforcing due to Grant's failure at the Tallahatchie. Sherman concluded that to delay the attack again would be too dangerous and decided to withdraw.[42]

Sherman ordered the army to withdraw during the late afternoon of 1 January 1863. Under the concealment of darkness the divisions withdrew to generally the same sites from which they had landed, leaving rear guard forces to protect the withdrawal. By daylight on 2 January the rear guards had reached the boat sites. Porter's gunboats were in position to cover the withdrawal of the steamboats from the rear of the column.[43]

The embarkation of Steele's force on the 30th had gone unnoticed by the Confederates and it was not until the evening of 1 January that they became alarmed that another attack was being prepared. Maury reinforced Withers's position at Blake's Levee with the 35th Mississippi, the 29th Louisiana, and the 23d Alabama. Lee believed an attack was imminent at Snyder's Bluff and quickly moved there with four of his regiments. At dawn on the 2d, it became clear to the Confederates that the Union army was no longer entrenched to their front and that the enemy may have shifted to attack at Snyder's Bluff. Maury alerted Withers to move to support Lee at Snyder's Bluff. As Maury got his force on the road he ran into Lee who was returning to the bayou area. Lee had seen no Union troops in front of Snyder's Bluff and was now convinced they had retreated. Lee and Withers gathered their forces and struck out to pursue Sherman's army. Withers took the 30th Mississippi, the 29th Louisiana, and the 23d Alabama and swept along the east side of the Chickasaw Bayou. Withers reached the Yazoo without any contact with an organized enemy finding only nine stragglers and the refuse of the Union army. Lee on the west side of the bayou pursued with his 2d Texas, and the 3d and 30th Tennesee Regiments. With the 2d Texas in skirmish lines, Lee found only the last remnants of two regiments drawn up as rear guard pickets. The 2d Texas reached the Yazoo and took the parting shots at the gunboats and troop steamboats as they headed out to the Mississippi River.[44]

On the morning of the 2d, Porter advised Sherman that McClernand had arrived down river and was waiting at the mouth of the Yazoo. Sherman hurried ahead with Porter and described to McClernand the state of the army and a summary of the battle. McClernand confirmed Sherman's suspicions that Grant was not coming to support the attack at the bayou. For the first time, Sherman found out what had happened to Grant.[45]

McClernand had finally arrived in Memphis on 28 December and had established immediate communications with Grant. McClernand found that Grant was establishing a new base of supply at Memphis and was opening the Memphis-Charleston Railroad from Grand Junction to that town. Grant anticipated a requirement to resupply and rearm Sherman completely from the Mississippi River and had completely stopped any efforts to put pressure on Pemberton in central

Mississippi. Grant's new plan after pulling back to the Tallahatchie was to embark his whole army on the river if necessary. When Sherman was fighting at the bayou, Grant had ceased to support the operation directly.[46]

Under these circumstances, McClernand and Sherman concluded that to continue the attack anywhere along the Yazoo would be futile. The army left the Yazoo and steamed to a rendezvous at Milliken's Bend on the 3d. On the 4th McClernand issued his first general order assuming command of the new Army of the Mississippi with two corps to be commanded by Sherman and Morgan.[47] In the one sided fight at the bayou Sherman's army had lost 208 killed, 1,005 wounded, and 563 missing. The Confederates had suffered only 57 killed, 120 wounded, and 10 missing.[48] The Chickasaw Bayou Campaign was over; the campaigns along the Mississippi had just started.

ENDNOTES

1. The War of Rebellion: A Compilation of the Official Records of the Union and Confederate Armies 128 vols. (Washington: Government Printing Office, 1880-1901) Series I, Vol. XVII, Part 1: 607. (Cited hereafter as OR).
2. Ibid., 607,622.
3. George W. Morgan, "The Assault on Chickasaw Bluffs" in

159

Battles and Leaders of the Civil War, Vol. III, Part II, ed. Robert U. Johnson, (New York: The Century Co., 1884), 465.

4. OR, Series I, Vol. XVII, Part 1, 638 and Morgan, 466.

5. OR, Series I, Vol. XVII, Part 1, 645, 682, 695.

6. Ibid., 655.

7. Ibid., 682.

8. lbid., 652.

9. OR, Series I, Vol. XVII, Part 1, 643 and Edwin C. Bearss, The Campaign for Vicksburg 3 vols. (Dayton, OH: Morningside House, Inc., 1985) 1: 197.

10. OR, Series I, Vol. XVII, Part 1, 92.

11. Morgan, 466.

12. Ibid., 466-467.

13. William T. Sherman, Memoirs of General W.T. Sherman (New York: The Library of America, 1990), 314.

14. OR, Series I, Vol. XVII, Part 1, 656.

15. Morgan, 467.

16. OR, Series I, Vol. XVII, Part 1, 649.

17. Ibid., 638.

18. Ibid., 688.

19. OR, Series I, Vol. XVII, Part 1, 656 and Bearss, 220.

20. OR, Series I, Vol. XVII, Part 1, 649-650.

21. Morgan, 468.

22. OR, Series I, Vol. XVII, Part 1, 652-653, 658-660 and

Bearss, 201.

23. <u>OR</u>, Series I, Vol. XVII, Part 1, 682,695.

24. Ibid., 644, 648.

25. Ibid., 682-683.

26. Henry A. Kircher, <u>A German in the Yankee Fatherland - The Civil War Letters of Henry A. Kircher</u> ed. Earl J. Hess, (Kent, OH: Kent State University Press, 1983), 47.

27. <u>OR</u>, Series I, Vol. XVII, Part 1, 640 and Morgan, 468-469.

28. <u>OR</u>, Series I, Vol. XVII, Part 1, 608, 628, 633.

29. Ibid., 633, 677.

30. <u>OR</u>, Series I, Vol. XVII, Part 1, 633-634 and Bearss, 192.

31. <u>OR</u>, Series I, Vol. XVII, Part 1, 633, 677-679 and Bearss, 192.

32. <u>OR</u>, Series I, Vol. XVII, Part 1, 661.

33. <u>OR</u>, Series I, Vol. XXII, Part 1, 633 and Henry C. Bear, <u>The Civil War Letters of Henry C. Bear: A Soldier in the 116th Illinois Volunteer Infantry,</u> ed. Wayne C. Temple (Harrogate,Tenn: Lincoln Memorial University Press, 1961), 24.

34. <u>OR</u>, Series I, Vol. XVII, Part 1, 633-634.

35. <u>OR</u>, Series I, Vol. XVII, Part 1, 609, 623 and <u>The War of Rebellion: A Compilation of the Official Records of the Union and Confederate Navies,</u> 31 vols. (Washington: Government Printing Office, 1894-1922) series I, Vol. XXIII: 587. (Cited

hereafter as <u>ORN</u>).

36. <u>OR</u>, Series I, Vol. XVII, Part 1, 676, 679.

37. <u>OR</u>, Series I, Vol. XVII, Part 1, 623 and <u>ORN</u>, Series I, Vol. XXIII, 588.

38. <u>ORN</u>, Series I, Vol. XXIII, 590 and OR, Series I, Vol. XVII, Part 1, 609.

39. Kircher, 50.

40. <u>OR</u>, Series I, Vol. XVII, Part 1, 609.

41. Ibid., 679.

42. <u>ORN</u>, Series I, Vol. XXIII, 597 and <u>OR</u>, Series I, Vol. XVII, Part 2, 609.

43. <u>OR</u>, Series I, Vol. XVII, Part 1, 609-610, 629, 632, 637 and <u>ORN</u>, Series I, Vol. XXIII, 598.

44. <u>OR</u>, Series I, Vol. XVII, Part 1, 684, 688-689 and Joseph E. Chance, <u>The Second Texas Infantry</u> (Austin, TX: Eakin Press, 1984), 90-92.

45. Sherman, 317.

46. <u>OR</u>, Series I, Vol. XVII, Part 2, 493-494, 501, 504, 508.

47. <u>OR</u>, Series I, Vol. XVII, Part 2, 530 and Sherman, 317.

48. <u>OR</u>, Series I, Vol. XVII, Part 1, 625, 671.

Note: The maps in Chapter Three and Four are derived from Bearss, 169, 184, and 192.

CHAPTER FIVE - CONCLUSION

In the final analysis several decisive factors at the strategic, operational, and tactical levels contributed to the outcome of the Chickasaw Bayou Campaign. At the Union strategic level the insertion of the amphibious force under McClernand decisively affected Grant's ongoing campaign in central Mississippi. At the Confederate strategic level, the reorganization of the command structure created the conditions which allowed the successful tactical reinforcement of the meager forces facing Sherman at the Chickasaw Bayou. At the operational level the twin confederate cavalry raids caused Grant to retreat rather than attack. Grant's retreat enabled Pemberton to focus all efforts and reinforcements against Sherman's forces at the bayou. At the tactical level, Sherman's forces wasted time and lacked a sense of purpose in the opening days of the battle. Morgan's blunders on the 29th sealed the Union fate. On the Confederate side, the battle was characterized by a strong sense of urgency and excellent generalship in the maneuvering of reinforcments.

At the strategic level, the Union command structure in the west was fractured and not designed to contribute to the necessary unity of effort to seize Vicksburg or, for that matter, accomplish anything else decisively. Grant had no authority at

163

all over forces supposedly moving from New Orleans, and had no control over forces just across the Mississippi at Helena. These problems were not critical to success or failure but simply set the stage for the real source of problem in the command structure. The designation of Major General John A. McClernand as commander of a separate amphibious army was a decisive factor in the campaign. The lack of a clear overall commander in the west allowed the imposition of this independent force into Grant's area of operations by Lincoln and Stanton. Grant felt compelled to stop a highly successful overland campaign in order to send his own amphibious force ahead of McClernand. Grant distrusted McClernand so much that this seemed his only solution to this situation. The impact of Grant's decision to stop his overland campaign became apparent to Grant only later when he found out the true nature of the Confederate retreat in the beginning of December. Grant said, "Had I known the demoralized condition of the enemy,... I would have been in pursuit of Pemberton while his cavalry was destroying the roads in my rear."[1] Had Lincoln and Stanton left Grant to his own devices, Grant's natural aggressiveness would have probably allowed him to find out about the enemy's condition in due time.

The Confederate reorganization of the command structure in the west significantly contributed to their tactical success at Chickasaw Bayou. Had the command system under which the Confederates fought the battle of Corinth been allowed to remain in place, the unity of effort that was critical to reinforce the small garrison at Vicksburg would have been absent. Under the earlier Confederate command structure, Braxton Bragg could not properly command two highly individualistic and antagonistic generals, Van Dorn and Price, from Chattanooga. Although Van Dorn was supposed to be in command in Mississippi, he did not have the formalities of rank or designated command, or the strength of will to unify the forces. The creation of a single command in the Mississippi area of operations under Lieutenant General John Pemberton, and the creation of the Western Theater command under General Joseph Johnston, significantly affected the campaign. As the clearly defined commander over Price and Van Dorn, Pemberton united the widely dispersed forces in Mississippi, stabilized the front in northern Mississippi, and heavily reinforced Vicksburg with the necessary artillery. Johnston provided the overall commander necessary to prioritize missions in the west and had the authority to shift forces to threatened regions. Between the two of them, a solid plan was developed at the strategic level for intra-theater reinforcement and a strategic cavalry raid. The planning conducted at the strategic level in these two areas was essential for success once the Union campaign against Vicksburg was initiated.

The most obvious and significant factors contributing to the outcome of the Chickasaw Bayou Campaign are at the operational level. Sherman's amphibious wing did a terrible job of concealing its activities. Porter's gunboats surged into the Yazoo River just days before the landing in order to clear landing sites. Porter had elements at the Yazoo for several months and could easily have established a pattern of activity which would have served less to highlight an impending assault and outline exactly where the landing would occur. As the steamboats with Sherman's force moved downriver, every hostile activity was met with looting and burning by the Union soldiers. Certainly some of these activities were spontaneous, yet for the most part they were encouraged throughout the chain of command. These depredations amply signalled the approach of the river force and characterized the lack of urgency displayed by Union forces throughout the campaign. If time was critical, the continuous unloading of troops to destroy property slowed the downriver movement unnecessarily. In the larger context of the campaign, these were not decisive factors because they could not be used by the Confederates to a significant advantage. The loss of surprise would only be important if Pemberton were able to reinforce Vicksburg. Otherwise, his forces at Vicksburg numbered only 6,000 men and were not expected to be much of an obstacle to Sherman's legion of 30,000 men. Success at Chickasaw Bayou required Grant to pin Pemberton's army in northern Mississippi in order to allow Sherman to attack the meager garrison at Vicksburg. The twin cavalry raids by Van Dorn and Forrest into Grant's rear were decisive factors to Union failure at the operational level. The two cavalry raids destroyed Grant's forward supply depot and his supply line to his logistics base in Kentucky. Grant said of these raids:

> Up to this time it had been regarded as an axiom in war that large bodies of troops must operate from a base of supplies which they always covered and guarded in all forward movements.[2]

At this stage in the war, Grant operated on the principles of war as he knew them. Sherman on the other hand spent a good deal of time thinking about future warfare and had already thrown out this axiom of war. As Sherman left Helena on 20 December and heard of Van Dorn's attack, he believed Grant was in no danger. Not only did he not believe in fixed supply lines, but he also had planned for resupplying Grant on the Yazoo River in just such an eventuality. Grant failed in his responsibilities by not pinning Pemberton along the front in northern Mississippi; in fact, Grant retreated. Pemberton was free to move his headquarters to Vicksburg and shift sizable forces from Price's army in front of Grant to the defense of

Vicksburg.

At the tactical level in the campaign, though the odds against success had begun to shift to the Confederacy, Sherman still had a tremendous advantage in time and troops available. As Sherman landed his forces on 26 December, no reinforcements had arrived from Pemberton's army. When Sherman landed on the 26th, he moved his army forward tentatively, allowing very small Confederate forces to stop his advance. Sherman's army should have overwhelmed those Confederate skirmishers and pressed the fight to the bayou. By the time Sherman's first forces reached the bayou in front of Walnut Hills on the evening of the 27th, Confederate reinforcements had begun to arrive. Sherman's army did not press the fight until the 29th and by that time the Confederate defenders had covered all the approaches necessary to cross the bayou. Sherman's failure as a commander was on the 26th and 27th as his army inched forward. The Confederates on the other hand reinforced at a frenzied pace, fought all available forces far in front of their defensive line, and showed a sense of urgency absent on the Union side.

A series of tactical mistakes by Brigadier General Morgan also contributed decisively to Union failure at the bayou. The only chance after losing the initiative to the Confederates was to gain a lodgement on Walnut Hills and overwhelm the defenders. Sherman still outnumbered the Confederates two to one and if he could have gotten Steele's reserve brigade on the top of the hills, he could have rolled up the line of hard pressed Confederates. Morgan's task, though not easy, was to make the initial penetration of the defensive line in the army's major attack on the 29th. Steele's mission was to attack through Morgan while all Confederate forces were pinned along the Walnut Hills defense line by the combined Union attacks. Morgan failed to carry pontoons forward as he had been ordered by Sherman and therefore lost the opportunity to bridge McNutt Lake at a point undefended by the Confederates. Two of Morgan's brigades could not cross over the bayou and attack due to this mistake. His next mistake was diverting Thayer's assaulting brigade as it deployed into the attack. Thayer's 4th Iowa had found a soft spot that, if exploited, would have penetrated the Confederate lines. The quick thinking Confederates plugged the gap as Thayer frantically searched the battlefield for his remaining regiments. Morgan was supposed to attack with four brigades directly supported by Blair's brigade on his left flank. Morgan's mistakes caused him to attack with only one of his four brigades.

The lack of success of the Chickasaw Bayou campaign forced both Grant and Sherman to make an assessment of the many mistakes that had been made. Sherman did not recognize his timidity on the 26th, 27th, and 28th. He believed instead that the battle was lost due to enemy reinforcements arriving from northern Mississippi, the inability to flank the defense line at Snyder's Bluff on 1 January, and Morgan's command failures during the main attack on the 29th.[3] Or the other hand Grant readily admitted his failure to grasp the army's ability to fight away from its base of supply. Grant's self assessment certainly contributed to his brilliant final campaign against Vicksburg in which success hinged on his operating without an established supply line. Grant's modification of his previous conception of the necessity to have unencumbered lines of supply was probably the most important product of the campaign.

The Confederates achieved only a partial success in the Chickasaw Bayou campaign and probably also learned the wrong lessons. The Confederates had been able to repulse Sherman, yet they failed to follow up and defeat him decisively. In central Mississippi Pemberton's army did not attempt to follow Grant's retreating army and thus lost an opportunity to strike an even more serious blow. The lack of a complete victory over Grant and Sherman enabled Union forces to renew their efforts against Vicksburg with vigor and without the true stigma of a defeat. The victory served to lull the Confederate leadership into a false sense of security about the way the battles for Vicksburg were to be fought in the future. Cavalry strikes on a grand scale were visualized as the solution to manpower shortages. The necessity to unify whole armies as Johnston had encouraged continued to be ignored as unnecessary. Finally, the Confederate leadership in Richmond concluded that Vicksburg really was a fortress and troops could easily defend it while bottled up in the city. The catastrophic loss of a whole Confederate army in Vicksburg on 4 July 1863 shows that success at Chickasaw Bayou may not have helped the Confederate cause.

ENDNOTES

1. U.S. Grant, <u>The Personal Memoirs of U.S.</u> Grant (New York: The World Publishing Co., 1952), 226.

2. Ibid., 220.

3. <u>The War of Rebellion: A Compilation of the Official Records of the Unior and Confederate Armies</u> 128 vols. (Washington: Governnent Printing Office, 1880-1901) Series I, Vol. XVII, Part 2: 588-589.

APPENDIX

ORDER OF BATTLE
DEC 1862

UNION WESTERN DEPARTMENTS:

```
                        WAR DEPARTMENT
                          HALLECK
    ┌──────────────┬───────────────────┬──────────────────┐
DEPARTMENT      DEPARTMENT          DEPARTMENT        DEPARTMENT
    OF              OF                  OF                OF
   OHIO          CUMBERLAND          TENNESSEE         MISSOURI
 (Wright)       (Rosecrans)          (Grant)          (Curtis)
```

GRANT'S DEPARTMENT:

```
                DEPARTMENT OF TENNESSEE
                        (Grant)
    ┌───────────┬────────────────┬──────────────┐
DISTRICT OF   DISTRICT OF      DISTRICT OF    DISTRICT OF
MEMPHIS       JACKSON          CORINTH        COLUMBUS
(Sherman)     (Hurlbut)        (Hamilton)     (Davies)
```

GRANT'S FIELD ARMY:

```
                ARMY OF THE TENNESSEE
                      (Grant)
                         |
                  XIII ARMY CORPS
                      (Grant)
       ┌─────────────────┬────────────┐
  Right Wing, XIII    Right Wing*   Left Wing
  Army Corps          (McPherson)   (Hamilton)
  (Sherman)
       |
  Three Divisions,
  Army of Tennessee
       |
  One Division,
  Dpt of Missouri
```

*NOTE: The name Army of the Tennessee was unofficial.
Officially the field army of the Department of the Tennessee
was the XIII Army Corps. Sherman commanded the designated

173

Right Wing of the Corps. Grant directly commanded McPherson and Hamilton in central Mississippi. When he corresponded with them he designated them his Right and Left wings, clearly meaning they held these wings in the main body of the XIII Army Corps in central Mississippi. Formalization of these units into properly designated corps would not happen until after the Chickasaw Bayou Campaign.

CONFEDERATE WESTERN DEPARTMENTS:

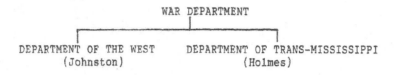

WAR DEPARTMENT

DEPARTMENT OF THE WEST   DEPARTMENT OF TRANS-MISSISSIPPI
      (Johnston)   (Holmes)

JOHNSTON'S DEPARTMENT:

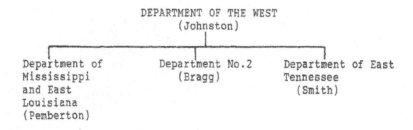

DEPARTMENT OF THE WEST
      (Johnston)

Department of   Department No.2   Department of East
Mississippi   (Bragg)   Tennessee
and East   (Smith)
Louisiana
(Pemberton)

PEMBERTON'S ARMY:

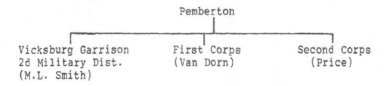

Pemberton

Vicksburg Garrison   First Corps   Second Corps
2d Military Dist.   (Van Dorn)   (Price)
(M.L. Smith)

174

ORDER OF BATTLE
CHICKASAW BAYOU

UNION AMPHIBIOUS FORCE – Right Wing, XIII Army Corps

    Maj. Gen. William T. Sherman

First Division-Brig. Gen. Andrew J. Smith

Escort- Company C, 4th Indiana Cavalry

    First Brigade-Brig. Gen. Stephen G. Burbridge

    16th Indiana Infantry,

    60th Indiana Infantry

    67th Indiana Infantry

    83d Ohio Infantry

    96th Ohio Infantry

    23d Wisconsin Infantry

    Killed: 5 Wounded: 16

    Second Brigade-Col. William J. Landrum

    77th Illinois Infantry

    97th Illinois Infantry

    108th Illinois Infantry

    131st Illinois Infantry

    89th Indiana Infantry

19th Kentucky Infantry

48th Ohio Infantry

Killed: 0 Wounded: 0

Artillery

Chicago Mercantile Battery (6 guns)

17th Company, Ohio Light Artillery (6 guns)

Killed: 0 Wounded: 0

SECOND DIVISION-Brig. Gen. Morgan L. Smith(w), Brig. Gen. David Stuart, Brig. Gen. Andrew J. Smith

First Brigade-Col. Giles Smith

113th Illinois Infantry

116th Illinois Infantry

6th Missouri Infantry

8th Missouri Infantry

13th U.S. Infantry(lst Battalion)

Killed: 15 Wounded: 63

Fourth Brigade-Brig. Gen. David Stuart, Col. T. Kilby Smith

55th Illinois Infantry

127th Illinois Infantry

83d Indiana Infantry

54th Ohio Infantry

57th Ohio Infantry

Killed: 12 Wounded: 39 Missing: 6

Artillery

Co.A, 1st Illinois Light Artillery (6 guns)

Co.B, 1st Illinois Light Artillery (6 guns)

Section, Co.H, 1st Illinois Light Artillery (2 guns)

Killed: 0 Wounded: 0

THIRD DIVISION-Brig. Gen. George W. Morgan

First Brigade-Col. Lionel A. Sheldon

118th Illinois Infantry

69th Indiana Infantry

120th Ohio Infantry

Killed: 0 Wounded: 27 Missing: 2

Second Brigade-Col. Daniel W. Lindsey

49th Indiana Infantry

7th Kentucky Infantry

114th Ohio Infantry

Killed: 17 Wounded: 68 Missing: 21

Third Brigade-Col. John F. DeCourcy

    54th Indiana Infantry

    22d Kentucky Infantry

    16th Ohio Infantry

    42d Ohio Infantry

    Killed: 48 Wounded: 321 Missing: 355

Artillery

    7th Company, Michigan Light Artillery (6 guns)

    1st Company, Wisconsin Light Artillery (6 guns)

    Killed: 2 Wounded: 12

Engineers

    Kentucky Company of Pioneers and Mechanics

    Killed: 0 Wounded: 0

FOURTH DIVISION-Brig. Gen. Frederick Steele

First Brigade-Brig. Gen. Frank P. Blair, Jr.

    13th Illinois Infantry

    29th Missouri Infantry

    30th Missouri Infantry

    31st Missouri Infantry

    32d Missouri Infantry

58th Ohio Infantry

4th Company, Ohio Light Artillery (6 guns)

Company C, 10th Missouri Cavalry

Killed: 99 Wounded: 331 Missing: 171

Second Brigade-Brig. Gen. Charles E. Hovey

25th Iowa Infantry

31st Iowa Infantry 3d Missouri Infantry

12th Missouri Infantry

17th Missouri Infantry

76th Ohio Infantry

Co.F, 2d Missouri Light Artillery (4 guns)

Killed: 6 Wounded: 21 Missing: 2

Third Brigade-Brig. Gen. John H. Thayer

4th Iowa Infantry

9th Iowa Infantry

26th Iowa Infantry

28th Iowa Infantry

30th Iowa Infantry

34th Iowa Infantry

1st Company, Iowa Light Artillery (6 guns)

Killed: 7 Wounded: 115 Missing: 2

Attached Cavalry

    6th Missouri Cavalry

    3d Illinois Cavalry

    Thielemann's Independent Cavalry Battalion, Companies A & B

    Killed: 2 Wounded: 3 Missing: 2

CONFEDERATE DEFENDERS - Second Military District

    Maj. Gen. Martin L. Smith(until 30 Dec.)

    Maj. Gen. Carter L. Stevenson

Barton's Brigade-Brig. Gen. Seth M. Barton

    40th Georgia Infantry

    42d Georgia Infantry

    43d Georgia Infantry

    52d Georgia Infantry

    Det.,Botetourt Virginia Artillery

    Killed: 15 Wounded: 39

Vaughn's Brigade-Brig. Gen. John C. Vaughn

    60th Tennessee Infantry

    61st Tennessee Infantry

62d Tennessee Infantry

Killed: 8 Wounded: 10

Gregg's Brigade-Brig. Gen. John Gregg

3d Tennessee Infantry

10th Tennessee Infantry

30th Tennessee Infantry

41st Tennessee Infantry

50th Tennessee Infantry

1st Tennessee Infantry Battalion

Killed: 1 Wounded: 3

Provisional Division- Brig. Gen. Stephen D. Lee

Brigade Commanders- Col. William T. Withers, Col. Allen Thomas, and Col. Edward Higgins

17th Louisiana Infantry

22d Louisiana Infantry

26th Louisiana Infantry

29th Louisiana Infantry

31st Louisiana Infantry

3d Mississippi Infantry

Companies A,D,E,G,I,L, 1st Mississippi Light Artillery

Company A, 14th Mississippi Light Artillery

Company I, 28th Mississippi Cavalry

Hill's Partisan Ranger Company

Killed: 33 Wounded: 67 Missing: 10

Unattached

Wirt Adam's Mississippi Cavalry Regiment

Troops Manning Vicksburg and late reinforcements Base Personnel

Company of Sappers and Miners

Detachment of Signal Corps

40th Alabama Infantry

1st Louisiana Heavy Artillery Regiment

8th Louisiana Heavy Artillery Battalion

27th Louisiana Infantry

1st Tennessee Artillery Regiment

Tracy's Brigade-Brig. Gen. Edward D. Tracy

(Arrived evening of 29th)

20th Alabama Infantry

23d Alabama Infantry

30th Alabama Infantry

31st Alabama Infantry

Maury's Division-Maj. Gen. Dabney H. Maury

      Hebert's Brigade-Brig. Gen. Louis Hebert

      (Reached Snyder's Bluff on 1 Jan)

      3d Louisiana Infantry

      21st Louisiana Infantry

      36th Mississippi Infantry

      37th Mississippi Infantry

      38th Mississippi Infantry

      43d Mississippi Infantry

      7th Mississippi Infantry Battalion

      Appeal Arkansas Battery

      Company H, 1st Mississippi Light Artillery

      Tobin's Tennessee Battery

Moore's Brigade-Brig. Gen. John C. Moore

      (Began to arrive afternoon 30 Dec)

      37th Alabama Infantry

      42d Alabama Infantry

      35th Mississippi Infantry

      40th Mississippi Infantry

      2d Texas Infantry

      Casualties for Base Troops and Reinforcements was one

Killed. That casualty was from the 2d Texas Infantry.

      NOTE: The order of battle at Chickasaw Bayou was

taken from Edwin C. Bearss, <u>The Campaign for Vicksburg</u> 3 vols. (Dayton,OH: Morningside House, Inc.) 1:224-229. For consistancy throughout the thesis only the unit designations from Bearss are used though they are not always the same as in the official records. Bearrs' order of battle reflects the most accurate unit designations derived from that author's extensive knowledge of the unit histories that are out of the scope of this work.

BIBLIOGRAPHY

Government Documents

War of the Rebellion: A Compilation of the Official Records of the Union and Confederate Armies. 70 vols. in 128 pts. Washington, D.C.: Government Printing Office, 1880-1901.

War of the Rebellion: A Compilation of the Official Records of the Union and Confederate Navies. 31 vols., Washington, D.C.: Government Printing Office, 1895-1927.

Periodicals and Articles

Brown, Alexander D. "Battle at Chickasaw Bluffs." Civil War Times Illustrated, 9 (1970): 44-48.

Colby, Carlos W. "Bullets, Hardtack, and Mud: A Soldiers View of the Vicksburg Campaign." Journal of the West, 4 (April 1965): 129-168.

Deupree, J.G. "The Capture of Holly Springs, Mississippi December 20, 1862." In Publications of the Mississippi Historical Society. Edited by Franklin L. Riley. Oxford, Miss.: Harrisburg Publishing Co., 1902: 51.

Hattaway, Herman. "Confederate Myth Making: Top Command and the Chickasaw Bayou Campaign," Journal of Mississippi History (November 1970): 311-326.

Hay, Thomas R. "Confederate Leadership at Vicksburg." In The Mississippi Valley Historical Review XI (March 1925): 543-560.

Kilmer, George L. "In March and Fight, Career of the Fifty Fifth Illinois under Sherman." Sketches of Federal Regiments. Washington, D.C.: American Press Ass.,1891: 125-127.

Lee, Stephen D. "Details of Important Work by Two Confederate Telegraph Operators, Christmas Eve,1862." Publications of the Mississippi Historical Society,Vol.VIII. Edited by Franklin L. Riley. Oxford, Miss.: Harrisburg Publishing Co., 1902: 52-54.

Lee, Stephen D. "The Campaign of General Grant and Sherman against Vicksburg in December 1862 and January 1st and 2d, 1863, Known as the 'Chickasaw Bayou Campaign'." Publications of the Mississippi Historical Society,Vol. IV. Edited by Franklin L. Riley. Oxford, Miss.: Harrisburg Publishing Co., 1902: 15-36.

Maury, Dabney H. "Van Dorn, The Hero of the Mississippi." In Annals of the War. Edited by Alexander K. McClure. Philadelphia: The Times Publishing Co., 1879: 461-465.

Morgan, G.W. "The Assault on Chickasaw Bluffs." Battles and Leaders of the Civil War,Vol.III. New York: The Century Co., 1884: 462-471.

Sherman, William T. "Vicksburg by New Year's." <u>Civil War Times Illustrated,</u> 16 (1978): 44-48.

Unpublished Materials

Committee of the Regiment. <u>Military History and Reminiscences of the Thirteenth Regiment of Illinois Volunteer Infantry.,</u> 1892.

Grecian, Joseph J. <u>History of the 83d Indiana Volunteer Infantry.</u> Cincinatti, 1865.

Hagerman, Edward H. <u>The Evolution of Trench Warfare in the American Civil War.</u> Ann Arbor, Michigan: University Microfilms International, 1985.

Other Sources

Bailey, George W. <u>A Private Chapter of the War.</u> St. Louis: G.I. Jones and Co., 1880.

Basler, Roy P., editor. <u>The Collected Works of Abraham Lincoln.</u> New Brunswick, N.J.: Rutgers University Press, 1953.

Bear, Henry C. <u>The Civil War Letters of Henry C. Bear: A Soldier in the 116th Illinois Volunteer Infantry.</u> Harrogate, Tenn.: Lincoln Memorial University Press, 1961.

Bearrs, Edwin C. <u>The Vicksburg Campaign,Vol. I.</u> Dayton,OH.: Morningside Press, 1985.

Bering, John A. <u>History of the Forty-Eighth Ohio Veteran</u>

Volunteer Infantry. Hillsboro,OH.: Highland News Office, 1880.

Bevier, Robert S. History of the First and Second Mississippi Brigades 1861-1865. St. Louis: Bryan, Brand and Co., 1879.

Boatner, Mark M. The Civil War Dictionary. New York: David McKay Company, Inc., 1959.

Bowman, S.M. and R.B. Irwin. Sherman and His Campaigns: A Military Biography. New York: Geo. C. Rand and Avery, 1865.

Boynton, H.V. Sherman's Historical Raid. Cincinnati, OH.: Wilstach, Baldwin and Co.,1875.

Cadwallader, Sylvanus. Three Years with Grant. New York: Alfred A. Knopf, 1956.

Calhoun, William L. History of the 42d Regiment Georgia Volunteers. Atlanta, GA.: Sisson, 1900.

Catton, Bruce. Grant Moves South. Boston: Little, Brown and Co., 1960.

Chance, Joseph E. The Second Texas Infantry. Austin, Texas: Eakin Press, 1984.

Committee of the Regiment. The Story of the Fifty Fifth Regiment Illinois Volunteer Infantry. Clinton, MA.: W.J. Coulter, 1887.

Committee of the Regiment. Regimental Association of the 49th Regiment Indiana (VOL) Infantry. Louisville, KY., 1895.

Cornwell, James M. Grant. New York: Van Nostrand Reinhold Co., 1970.

Department of History, USMA. The American Civil War. West Point: Government Printing Office, 1977.

Fieberger, G.J. Campaigns of the American Civil War. West Point,NY.: Military Academy Printing Office, 1910.

Fiske, John. The Mississippi Valley in the Civil War. Boston and New York: Houghton, Mifflin and Co., 1900.

Grant, U.S. Personal Memoirs of U.S. Grant. Cleveland and New York: The World Publishing Co., 1952.

Hartje, Robert G. Van Dorn. Charlotte, N.C.: Vanderbilt University Press, 1967.

Hattaway, Herman. General Stephen D. Lee. Jackson,Miss.: University Press of Mississippi, 1976.

Hattaway, Herman and Archer Jones. How The North Won. Chicago: University of Illinois Press, 1983.

Hopkins, Owen J. Under the Flag of the Nation - Diaries and Letters of a Yankee Volunteer in the Civil War. Columbus, OH.: Ohio State University Press, 1961.

Johnston, Joseph E. Narrative of Military Operations during the Civil War. New York: Dacapo Press, 1959.

Jones, Archer. Confederate Strategy from Shiloh to Vicksburg. Baton Rouge, LA.: Louisiana State University Press, 1961.

Kircher, Henry A. A German in the Yankee Fatherland: The

Civil War Letters of Henry A. Kircher. Kent, Ohio: Kent State University Press, 1983.

Larke, Julian K. General Grant and his Campaigns. New York: J.C. Derby and N.C. Miller, 1864.

Lewis, Lloyd. Sherman Fighting Prophet. New York: Harcourt, Brace and Co., 1932.

Liddell Hart, Basil H. Sherman: Soldier, Realist, American. Westport,Conn.: Greenwood Press, 1978.

Marshall, Thomas B. History of the Eighty Third Ohio Volunteer Infantry. Cincinnati, Ohio: The Eighty Third Ohio Volunteer Infantry Ass., 1913.

Maury, Dabney H. Recollections of a Virginian in the Mexican, Indian, and Civil Wars. New York: Charles Scribner's Sons, 1894.

McDonough, James L. Shiloh - in Hell before Night. Knoxville: The University of Tennessee Press, 1977.

Miers, Earl S. The Web of Victory. New York: Alfred A. Knopf, 1955.

Morris, William H. Infantry Tactics, Vol. I. New York: D. Van Nostrand, 1865.

Pemberton, John C. Pemberton, Defender of Vicksburg. Chapel Hill, N.C.: University of .forth Carolina Press, 1942.

Porter, David D. Incidents and Anecdotes of the Civil War. New York: D. Appleton and Co., 1891.

Porter, David D. The Naval History of the Civil War. New York: The Sherman Publishing Co., 1886.

Sandburg, Carl Abraham Lincoln - The War Years. New York: Harcourt, Brace and Co., 1939.

Sherman, William T. Memoirs of General William T. Sherman. New York: The Library of America, 1990.

Simon, John R., ed. The Papers of Ulysses S. Grant, Vol.3 and Vol.4. Carbondale, Ill.: Southern Illinois University Press, 1972.

Wheeler, Richard. The Siege of Vicksburg. New York: Thomas Y. Crowell Co., 1978.

Williams, Kenneth P. Lincoln Finds a General, Vol.4. New York: The MacMillan Co., 1956.

Wilson, James H. The Life of John A. Rawlins. New York: The Neale Publishing Co., 1916.